ALTERED TAROT

the end

of

love

by r. tanksley

photography
by k. hiatt

Unencumbered Press

THE END OF LOVE published by:
Unencumbered Press
Portland, Oregon

ISBN 979-8-9865664-0-5 Trade Paperback
ISBN 979-8-9865664-3-6 Trade Paperback
ISBN 979-8-9865664-3-6 eBook

ALTERED TAROT

the end

of

love

to my twin flame, Fabian
you taught me
how to love
myself
in gratitude, my love
—r. tanksley

to the shadows and to the light —k. hiatt

Trigger Warning

This book contains references to domestic violence including emotional abuse, physical violence, sexual violence, and psychological aggression. Please exercise discretion and healthy self-care.

Contents

Reasons/Causes

The Future

The Basic Five Card Tarot Spread

- is used to determine a course of action

- reveals insights, and the likely outcome

- unearths hidden potential in the situation

Card 1

3 of Swords

Card 2

10 of Swords

Card 3

The Moon

Card 4

The High Priestess

Card 5

The Star

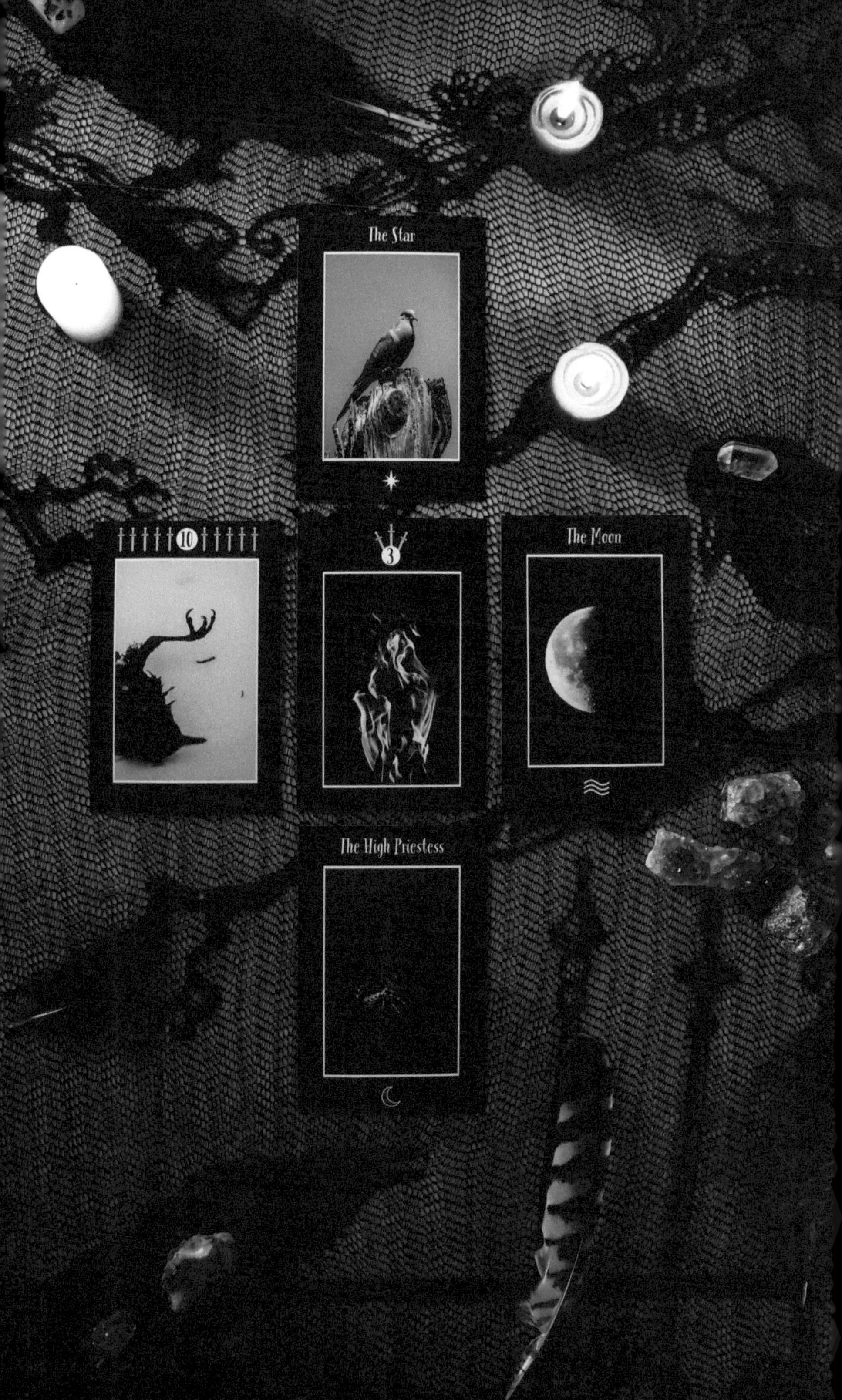

The Star
The Moon
The High Priestess

The Present Situation

*This card represents the present
situation of the querent.*

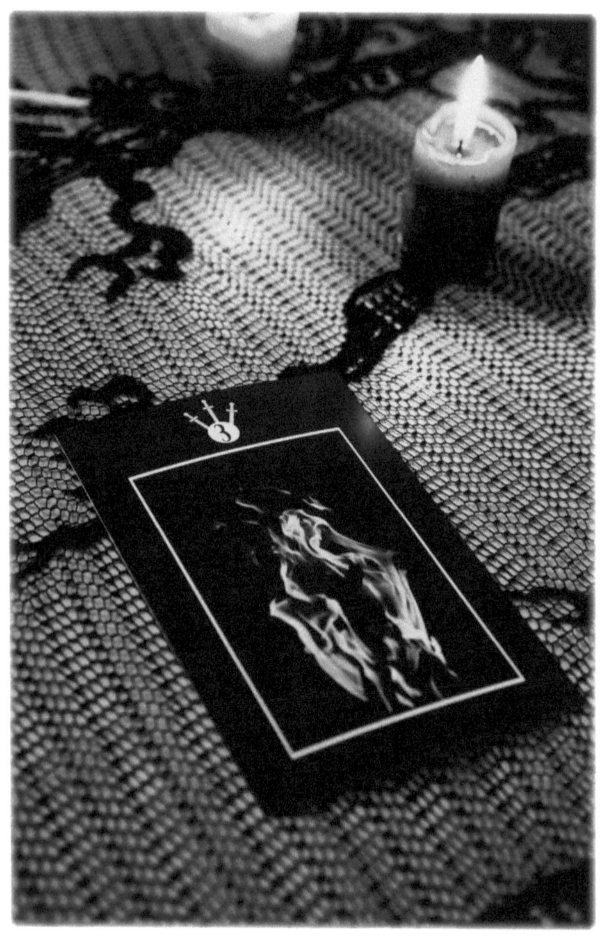

3 of Swords

a significant separation or breakup

intense loss and grief

the ending of a draining and frustrating situation

enduring suffering to find deeper meaning

a time to become free again

witnesses your pain

implores you to let go of a relationship
that didn't live up to its promises

asks you to dig deeper, perhaps
to the depths of your soul

resilience as the heart does not truly break

healing as the swords point down, the
damage is done, they are at rest

asks you to forget your past and prepare for
what is approaching, the next stage of your life

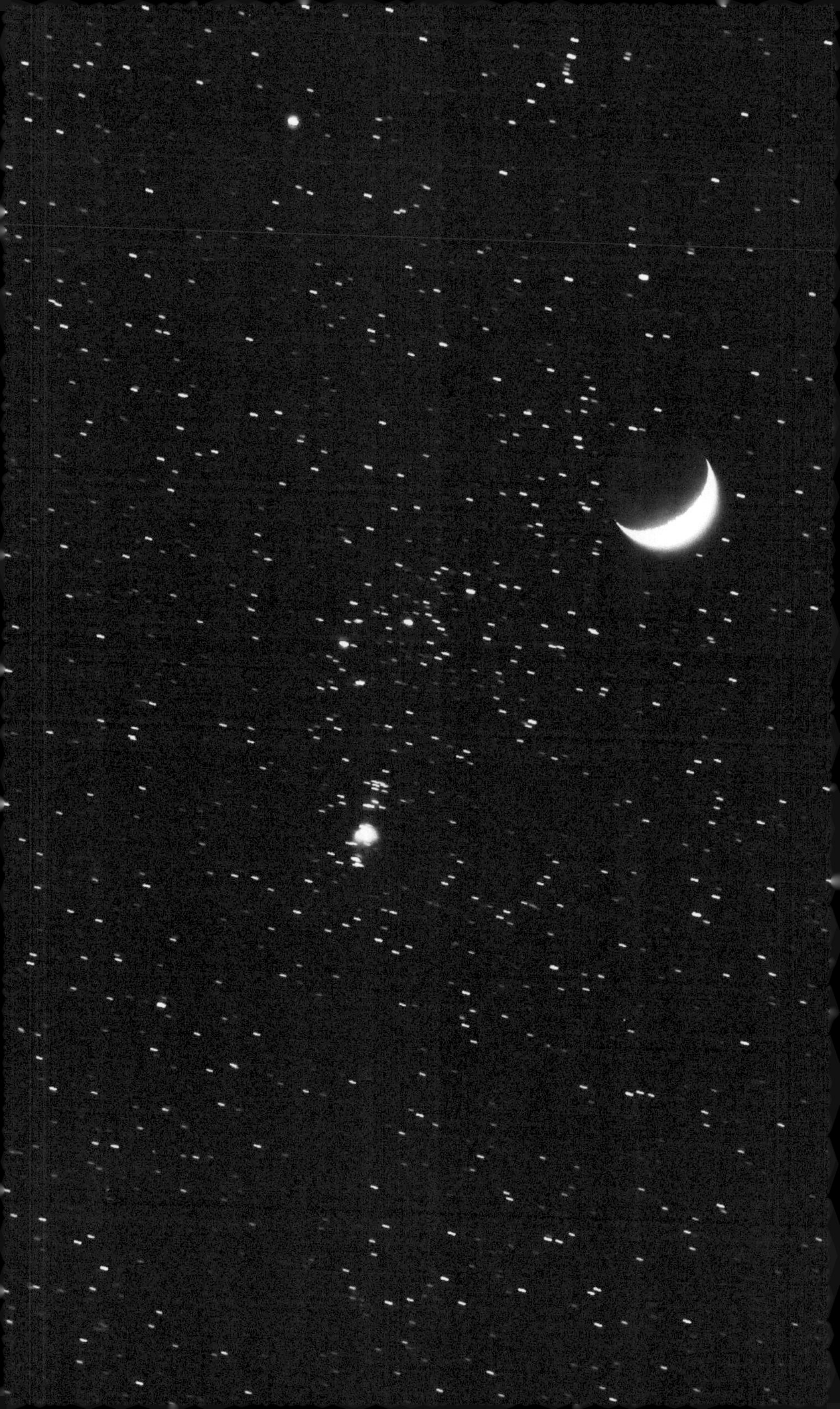

The Past

This card reveals past events that are still having an influence on the current situation.

These may need to be let go of in order for the situation to reach its full potential, shown in card 5.

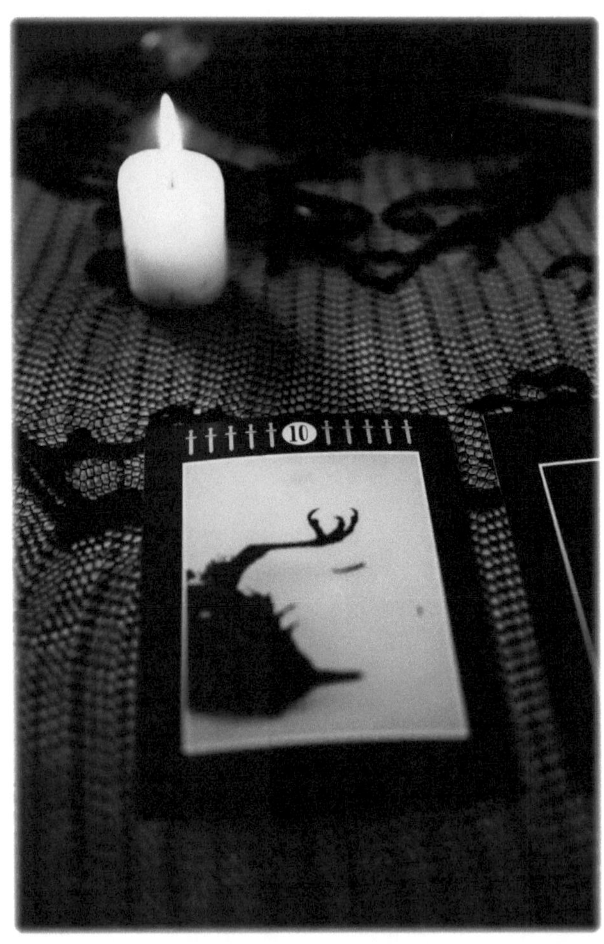

10 of Swords

force of extreme magnitude

finality, the ending of something

a time of suffering, bitterness, grief, and pain

betrayal

limit reached, line crossed

there are things beyond our ability to change

the situation is unavoidable

accept the inevitable end

closing of an exceptionally tough chapter in life

paradoxical sense of relief, there is no going back

rock bottom is a springboard

Weight

The weight of my love
a burden
Difficult to carry
Trudging   you climb
I climb
The weight of your grace
Our balancing
Act of despair
Where does love end
and accountability begin
What behavior denotes love
What behavior negates it
Impermanent
and permanent
Like the wind
there
Scream the word roots
Even as I fly off
Into the black.

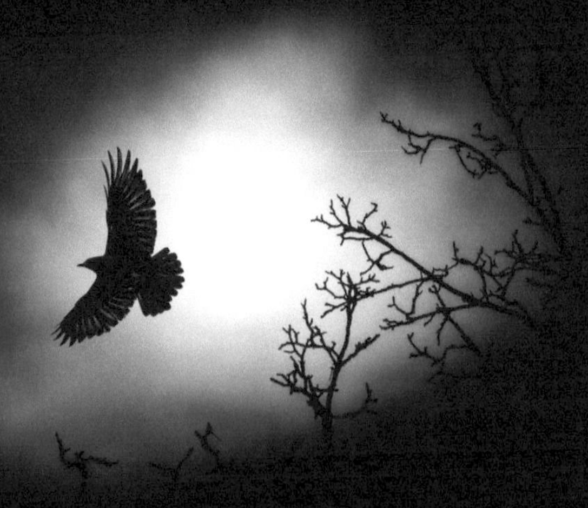

Resilient?

I don't know
What the term
Resilient means
Still breathing
If I can feel
Pain
Am I still here?
Here meaning present
Or my mind   blank
Parallel to my body

A body touched
Is it still mine?
How many breaths
Required to erase
~~Forceful touches~~
Does my mouth still speak

No consent override
The space surrounding
My body
I am resilient?
Because it does not
Belong to me.

Land of Disenchantment

You are flawed
Loving you
is flawed
And by flawed
I mean
Air to breathe
That I cannot breathe in
without pain

Why would you want
This for me
Or you saw
I had no choice
And simply followed
Questions I have
warning
What was the warning
Was it there and I simply
Didn't see

Is this a punishment for
Wrongdoings in a former life
Is this a reward
What is this
Strange painful domicile
That nourishes me
Land of disenchantment
Where you and I live
And love

I am practicing a way
To breathe
That doesn't make you angry
Can you see me here
Under this halo
Or only the reflection
of your ideas
That insist on shadowing
My shadow.

Refraction

Lift the veil white
Fog clears to
Definition of
A mirror not empathy
Through my features
I read your
Flaws like a bible
A crucifixion a rising
The following/the benediction

Affix this lens
Refraction
Watch you
Grow and shrink
in proportion
To my love

The typical oxygen
in lungs water
To thirsty roots

My tears
Play your strings
The grief inside me
Your song of sadness
Blue waves of cloud
Rolling
Between us
as I kneel
Before it
So shall you.

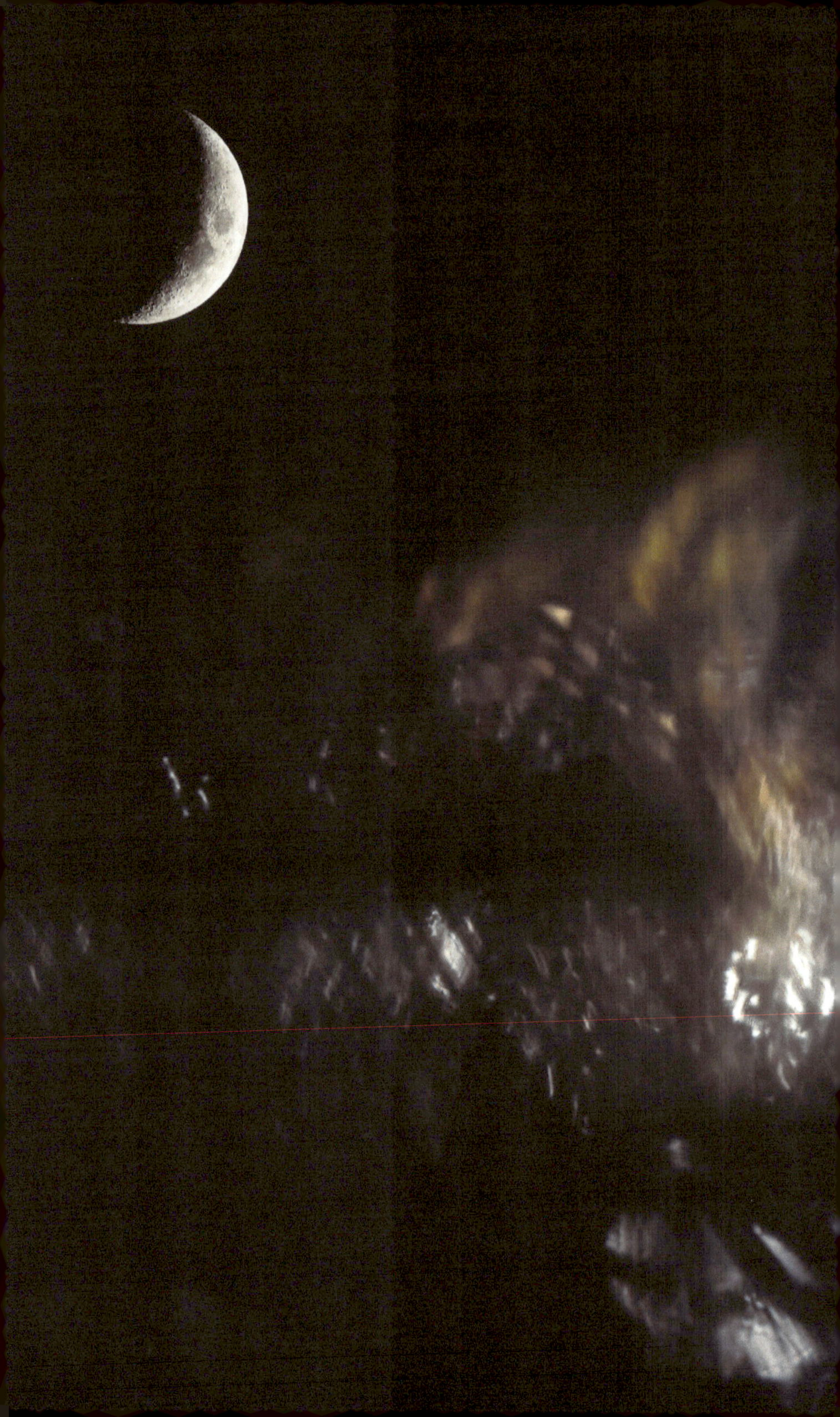

Illusion

Brushstrokes
Colors of your choosing
How you paint me
Manifesting
Your own pain
in art.

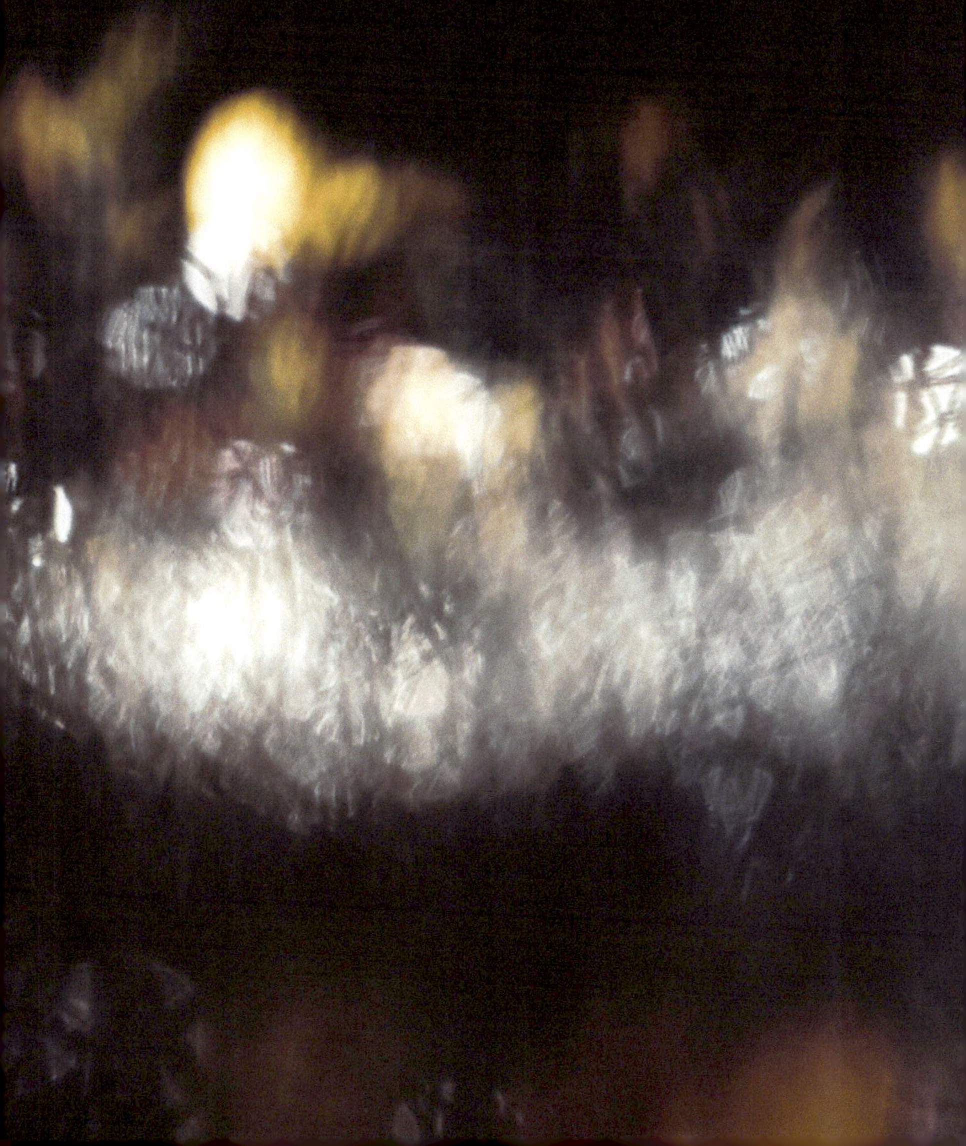

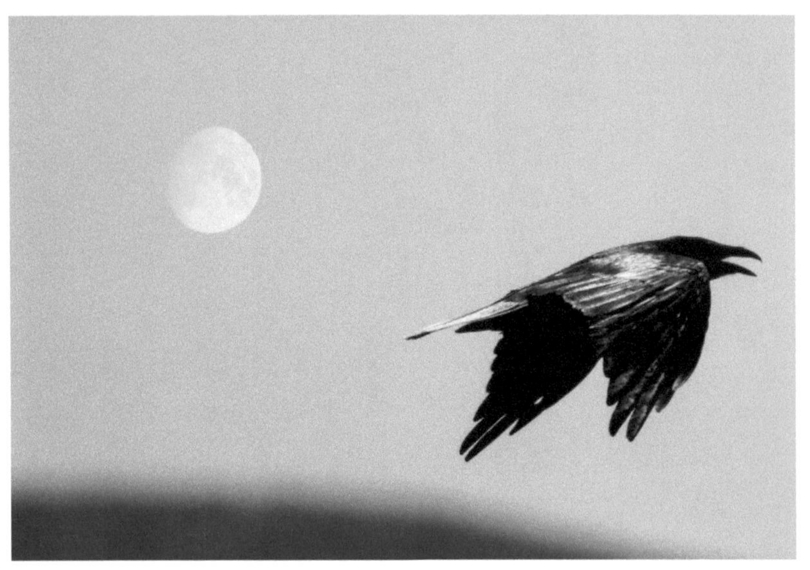

Line

A scribbled note
Describing your wrongs
A line etched in sand
and then pondered
Will I let the wind erase
What I value above all else
or will I fill the line
With dripping cement
Mixed with tears and minerals
From the earth
The earth
I too would harden into concrete
The line, my eyes, tears
Other things that once belonged to me.

Obsidian

One day perhaps
I will awaken to birdsong
And emerge reborn
Young trees and plants
Growing
Over the volcano now dormant
Black obsidian

Replenishing the soil
That once was the lava flow
of my anguish
Perhaps here
You will finally teach me
How to plant

Or yet
Hoping
For the true ending
Prematurely
An end to the clinging
Suffocation
of servitude
Attaining true freedom
Flight
From the same roots
I cannot grow
or find

What made you
change your mind
My flaws
Singing out loud
To yours.

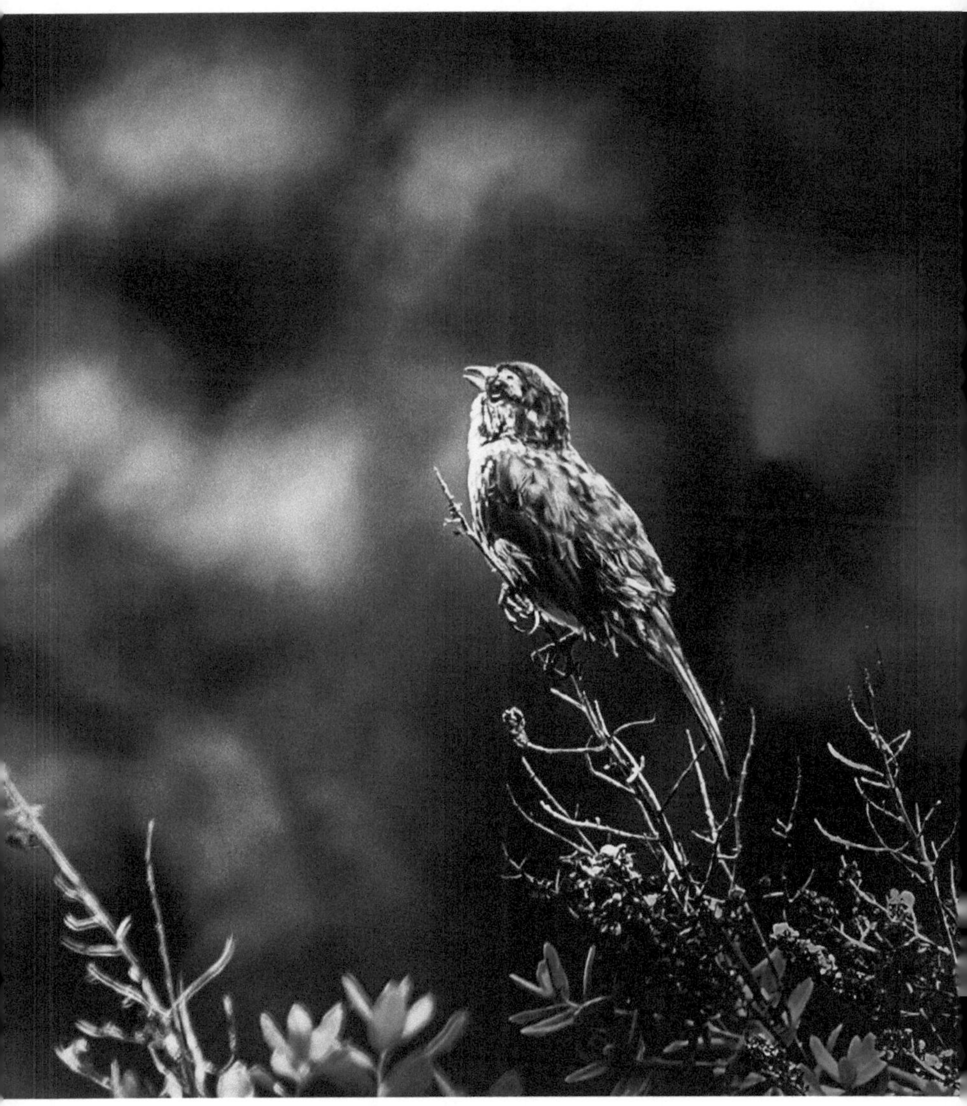

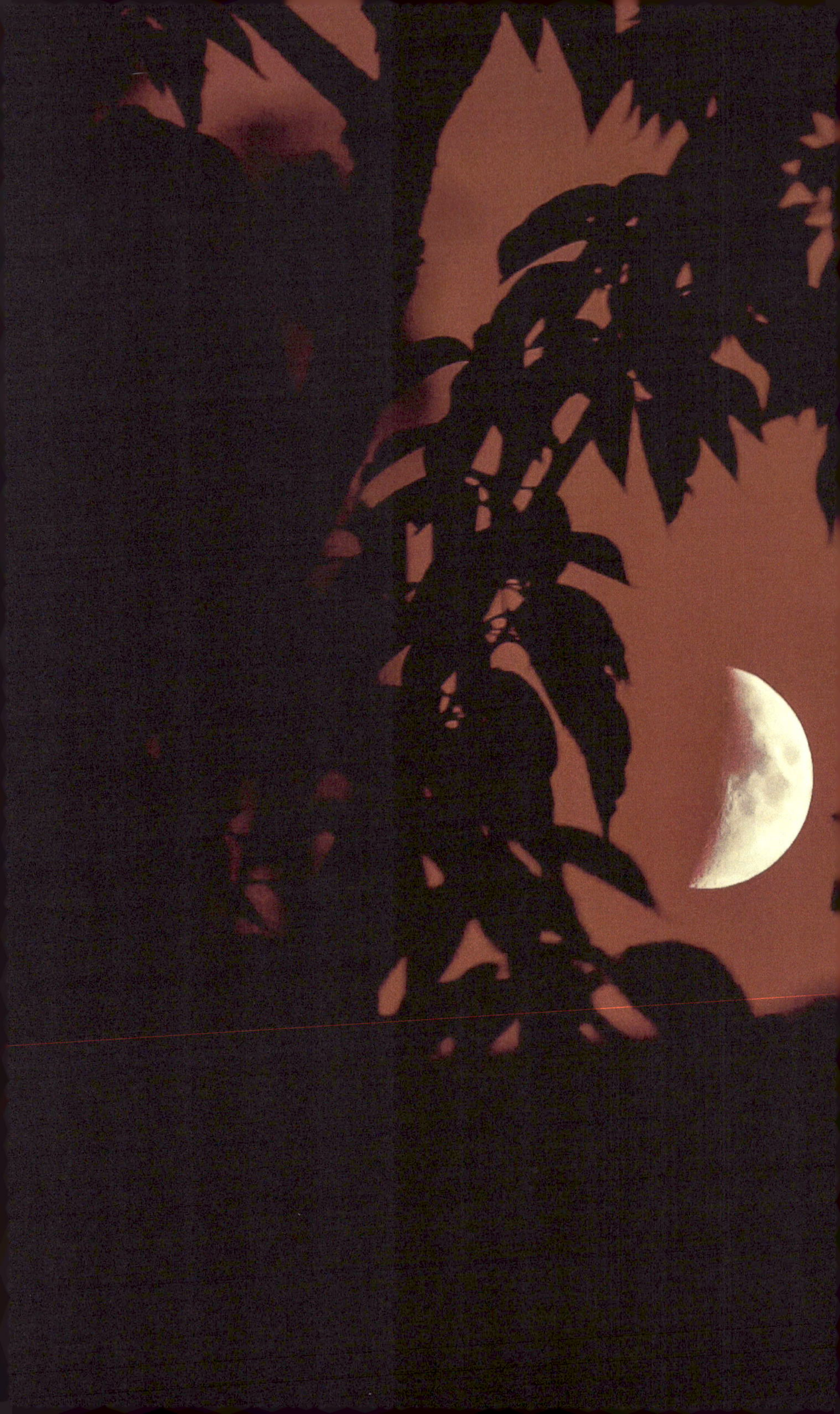

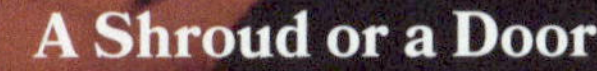

A Shroud or a Door

The moon rising
behind
The voice
I love so
Through the crystals
In the air
A complicated star
With a black and gold corona
Throbbing and beckoning
Winking hydrogen
Burning

Red light
Followed by blackness
A shroud
or a door
Depending
Thin skin thickens
More space
for you to erase.

Unsung

The ripple
of the rope
Sinewy
Winding from the heart
To the tendons in the wrist
a slow burning
Running through
Rising and falling
Shaping my anger

The broken ax
used to free you
From the metal trap
Cracked teeth
That gnawed the rope
Binding limbs

Now you run free
Over me
Waving my scars like medals
You earned in battle
Making one new cut
each time
I cry for justice

Days and days
Will go by
Wearing down my resistance
Will to oppose
Sold for the price of
Better than loyalty

All hail
The mighty one
Collector of stories
Blood and bones
I knelt here
Why me
Why me
Why me

Trembling
I will crawl
Back into my bed
of night
Wax and wane

Unsung
Silent radiance
Amidst
Clusters of forgiveness.

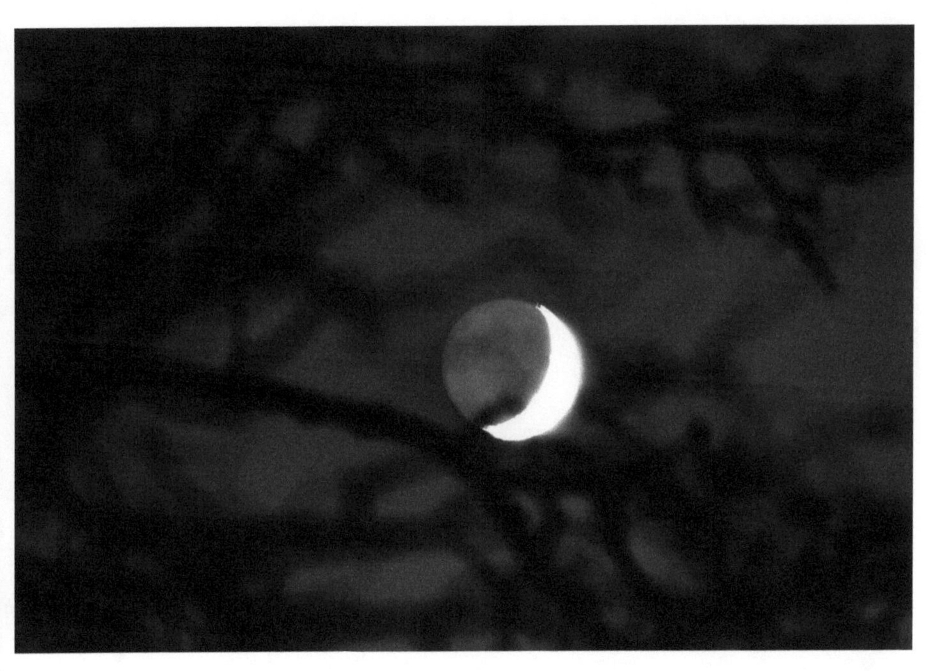

What Else Would You Like

What else would
You like my life
Wrapped up
Given
My autonomy
thoughts words feelings
Yours to sift and sort
Through organized
by your desire
to control
My silence
Take what you like
Please the rest
Discard abuse
punish reshape
You choose.

Trim Wings

Licensure
To do as you please
Upturned roots
I'm sure I've thought
Of all this before
Now your prison
The bindings
meant for me
Tattoo the mark
into my skin
Rearrange letters
in an order
To please you
Remove faces
Trim wings
Names places
Trim wings
Dates and times
Melodies turned off
Silent worship
At your feet
The thick ooze
of compliance.

Don't I Love You

I am willing
To hurt myself
To teach you
Why do I have to
Do this for you
Crucify me
For your own gains
Days going
by in a blur
Losing track of time
and space
Build a fire for me
Hold my hands
in the flames
If I do it for you
Don't I love you
Break myself
Against your
Brick and mortar
When I shatter like glass
Stomping on my shards
Your cruel feet
Grinding me to dust.

Consideration

You talk about
Consideration
Like I should
Be grateful
You make rules
for the things
I ask
Even though
I say nothing
You dictate
Our time together
But don't give me
What I ask
of our time
Together
You tell me
It's not my day
But it is
It is.

Flightless Safety

Go backwards
Devolve
Into something that can
Love you again instead
Woken
Spit out
Onto the riverbank

Refuse nourishment
Take apart my shelter
Stick by stick
Woven threads
I pick apart in my sleep
rivlets of
river water I am
No longer
Immersed in
tears
Extinguishing the slight embers
coaxed by
faultless devotion

Sew up tight
The body bag
Alive inside
I try to die for you
Here I will stay
Flightless safety
Unexposed to the elements.

Praise

The only praise
I can wear
is the one you deem
The crown
You put on my head
The flowers you deliver
The titles you bestow

Too bright
Too much
More of this
Less of that
Wants needs
Wants needs
Change
No change
Words at your disposal
Used too freely
Losing meaning
and shape
Debilitated

You say you love me
But really you
Want to control me
Take the things you need
Keep me on my knees
Filter inputs
Control outputs
Is guarded love, love
Is measured love, love
Is intention to love, love.

Strain to Hear

With eyes that don't
See right
Angles of black and white
Instead adapted to
True latitude

The full spectrum of
Ultraviolet light
particles take shape
my thoughts sewing
fragments reconstructing
Framing blindness
In the mind's eye

How to listen
To the words not spoken
Sounds not made
I strain to hear
Thread
Illuminated silvery
Lost in the wind
of intrusion

Unused wings
Scar tissue
old wounds stretched
unfolded slowly
painfully
bird
Feathers rustling
Or angel.

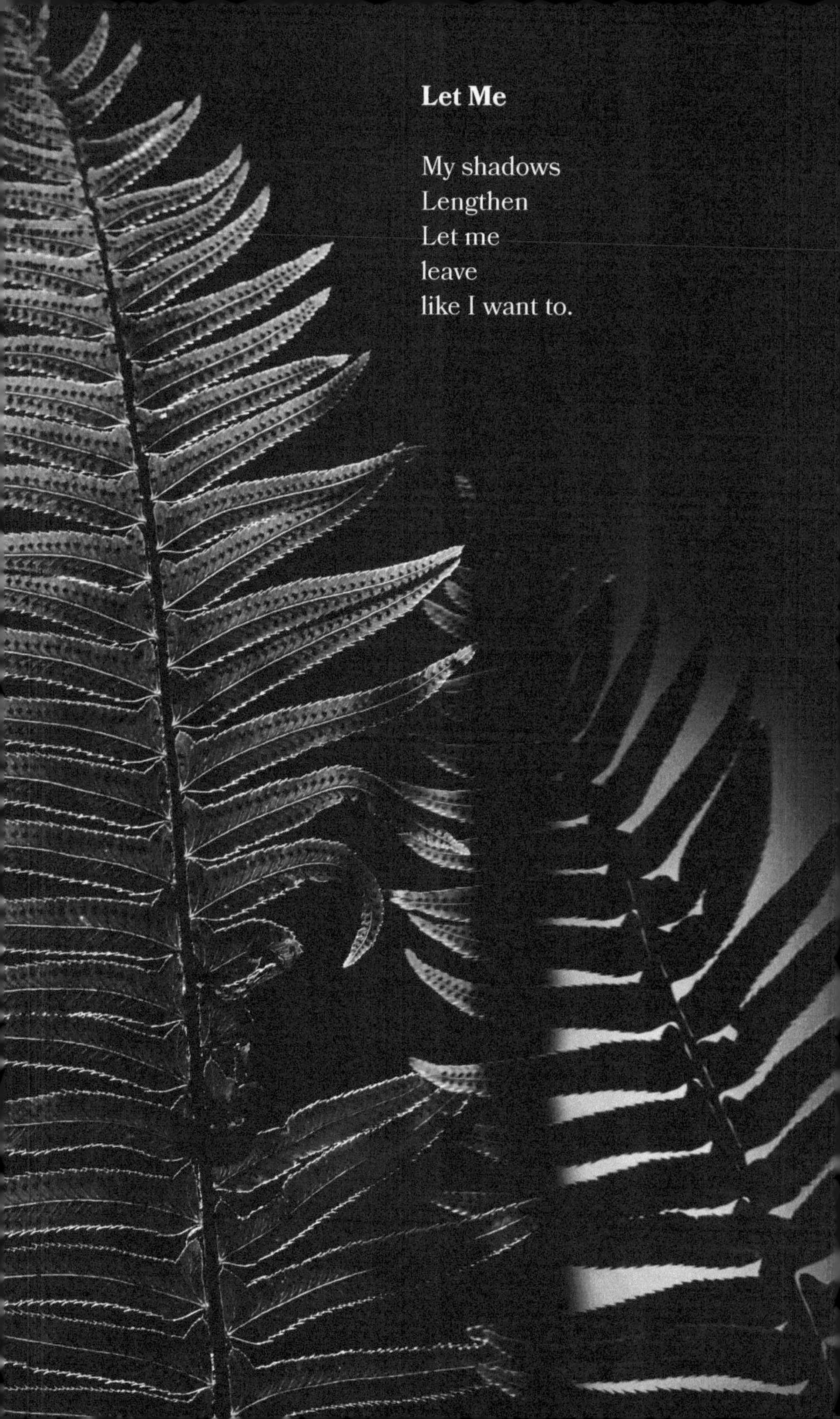
Let Me

My shadows
Lengthen
Let me
leave
like I want to.

My shadows
Lengthen
Let me
leave
like I want to.

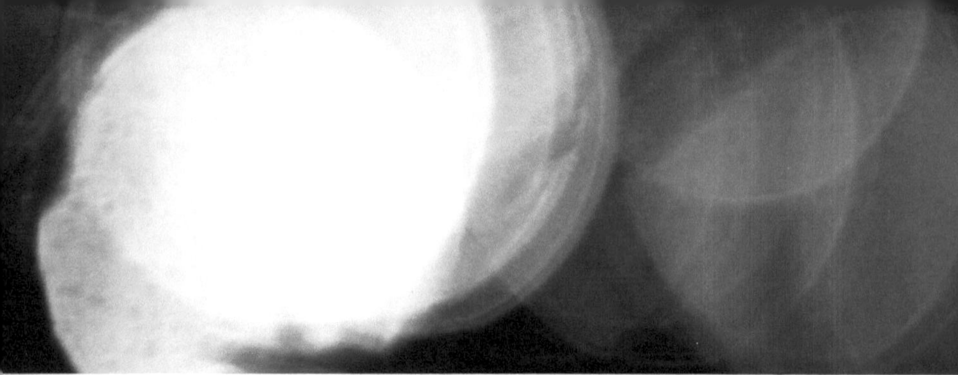

Projection

Cut me into
pieces fractions
Take the one
displeasing you
Record it
Choose a name
From the list your mother
Provided for women
Who misbehave

Name the piece
Say it loud
Louder
Make sure everyone
Can hear you

Once you have
An audience
Punish the piece
You cut
Twist it make
It cry out

Choose a primal fear
From the list your sergeant
Provided for women
Who misbehave
Shove it into the piece
Control it
String it up
Write your own name
Manipulator
on its chest

Bow to your audience
Return to the
remaining
pieces fractions
Cry with them over the
disobedient piece
Gather the pieces into
A new fractured whole

Repeat
Until there is
None
of me left.

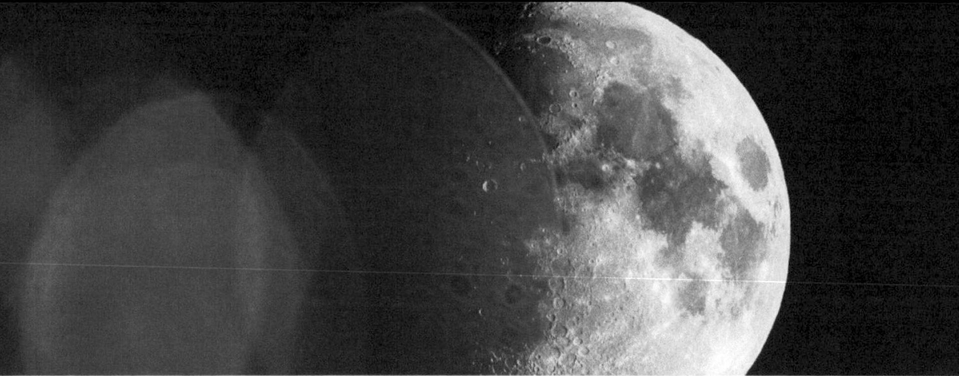

Restraint

You ask for
Restraint obliging
Cut out my tongue
Demanding
Me to speak
Bind
my hands
Crying
For my touch

Not shadows
beautifully darkened
By grief
and time not
a heart
Aching or loved not
Wounded ego
Or fallen pride
No emotion named

The moon rarely
Gives up
As she is patient
And all serving
But the reckoning
Rising tide.

Clear Choices

Beyond I cried
My tears prized
Marked and collected
Brought to you
by your ancestors
Laying your head back
You drink them
Restarting your stalled heart
Expanding collapsed lungs
Blood flowing
Giving you life
Arousal
My grief fills
You with life
I can't love another
Water tells the story.

Flight

What does a lie look like
Black uncurling
Dripping
I am not
Leaving
Again
No matter what
I am
Leaving

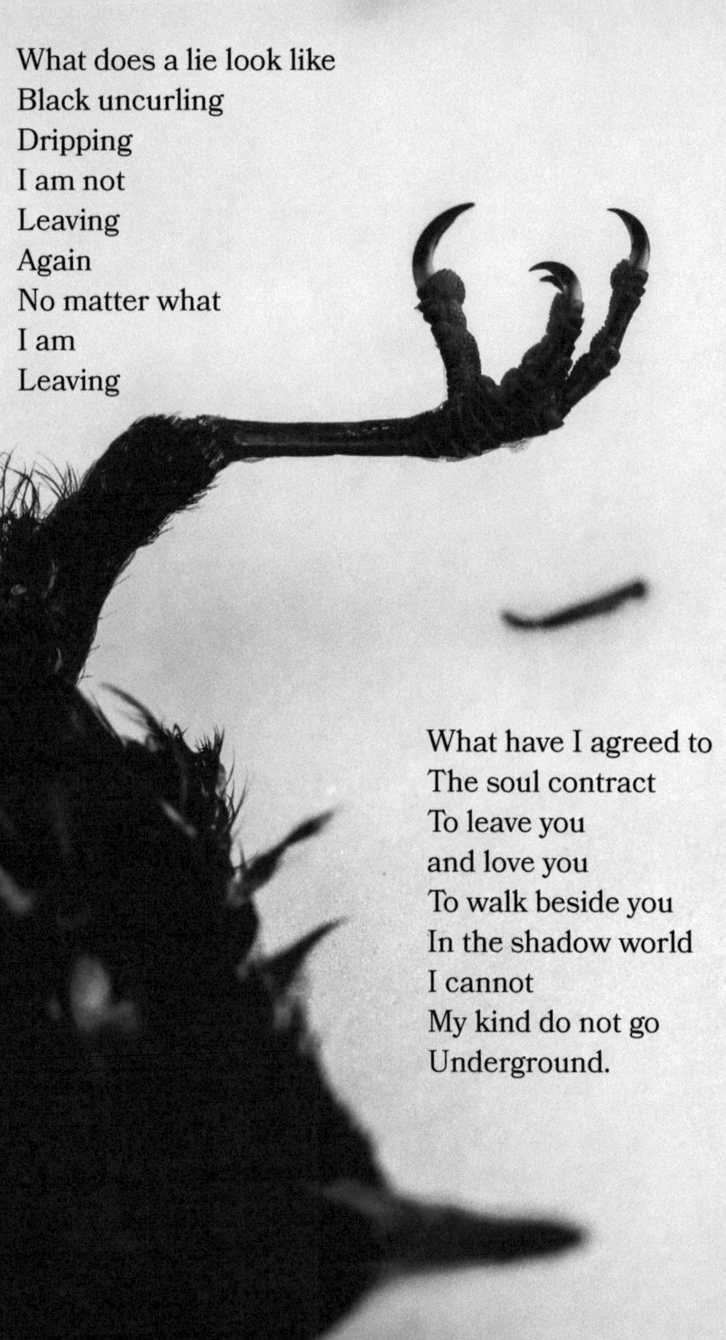

What have I agreed to
The soul contract
To leave you
and love you
To walk beside you
In the shadow world
I cannot
My kind do not go
Underground.

Rootless

Return to the cliff top
Heights
Full circle
You who I met
on my travels
Are no longer here
I can see
Everything
The forest below
The ocean distant
Where I last saw you

I can see
I am alone here
With the wind
Stars and moon
and knowledge
The inky snake
of knowing
No one is enough
What is to be my food
What is to be my life
Empty
Rootless
Floating
Distant
Radiant.

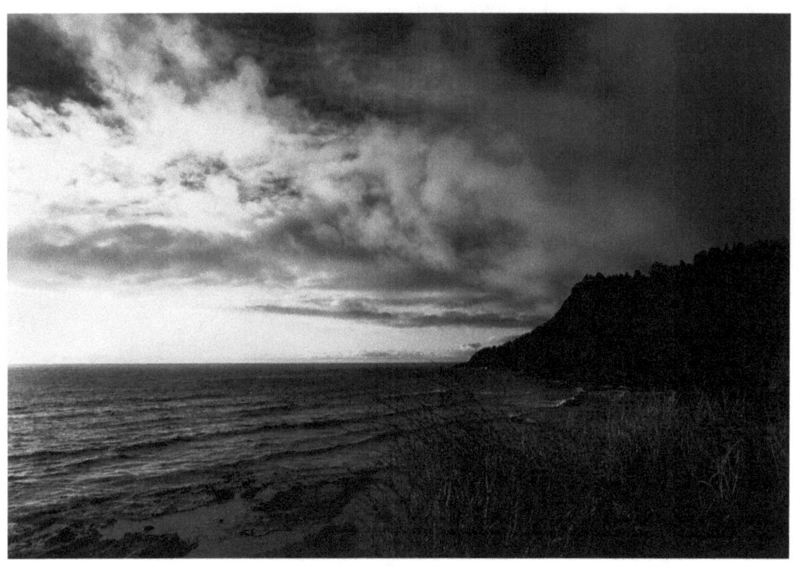

Reasons/Causes

This card reveals the reasons/causes that led to the querent's current situation.

It may reveal any obstacles that are standing in the querent's way and works in conjunction with card 2.

If there is a strong correlation between these two cards the querent must work on what is shown by them to reach the potential shown in card 5.

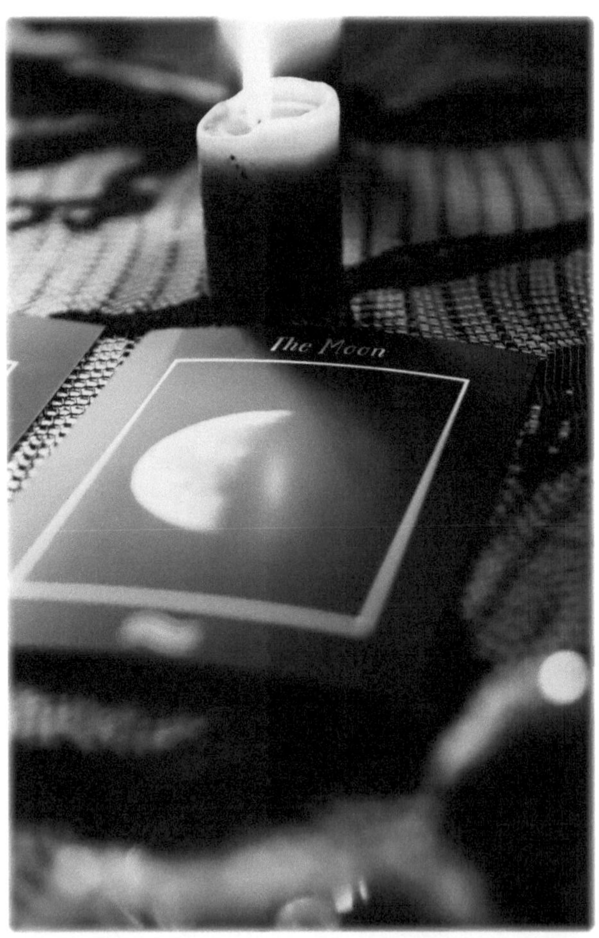

The Moon

your higher self is calling you

your spiritual birth

a new path is calling you

search for the hidden forces that must be unraveled

take off the mask and accept the truth

negativity, deep memories, and fears must be let go

let your wolf howl

be open to the gray areas, the
swirling nature of truth

an ultimate test of the soul's integrity

Tearing

The unwillingness
Fear of loving
Oneself
Completely
Tearing in resistance
to faith
Defiling love
carried across lifetimes
Will you
Realize
you are servicing
Our ending.

Only My Bones

Sudden retreat
From
Shared struggle
Leaving me
to fight
for our souls
You run and I am
Reflected light
Only
My bones
Upon
Your return
To cradle.

Transfigured

Transfigured
After your tearing
Half of me
Doesn't know
how to behave
I can cut
Worthwhile pain
After all ending
Long term learning
What is
One life out of
Many
I can wait.

Sacred Space

New Moon
After blows are dealt
faith is learned
The sacred space
Once denied
won in battle
Unlit
emotions cross
A face you cannot see
Screaming so forlorn
It merges with the silence
Unheard.

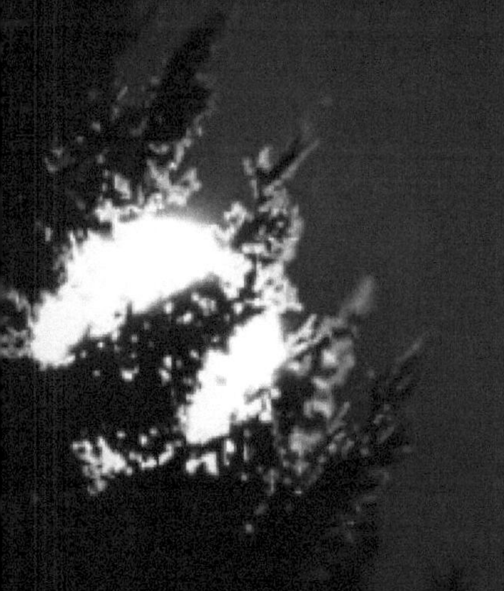

Divine Feminine

I have been
Through many
Battles
None like this
Grief as food
Sustenance for love
Pangs
My sadness feeds you
Fuels you
to hurt me
even more
This has an expiration
As I'm sure
You know
But the cause
For concern
My line
Lack of any line
When did I decide
Unconditional love
Meant you could take
Whatever you needed
Unconditional
Means no conditions
How does it exist
Synonymous
with healthy boundaries
Trust the divine
They say
and so my sorrow
Drink up
While I look to the sky.

Faltering

Faltering
There could be
an opening light
seeping the silence
when the wave
Washes over
Filling my mouth
Softness slips through
my fingers
I wait
for respite
For you
From you.

Rainstorm

Rainstorm
Malevolent
Stir me up
Watch me come
Crashing down
Give me an ax
and I will chop
Give me a chain
and I will bind
Love me and I will
Shatter like glass
in your hands

When you were gone
I danced
in the rain
The air
Cold
and motionless
But I could
Even so
move hands
that were not
Holding you

Flood
of tears, rain, emotion
All the things
That come back to me
On the tide

Words hang in the air
Cumulonimbus clouds
the backdrop
to our dissonance
I patiently wait
For the beauty
Wonder
Ephemeral vibrancy
of your rainbow.

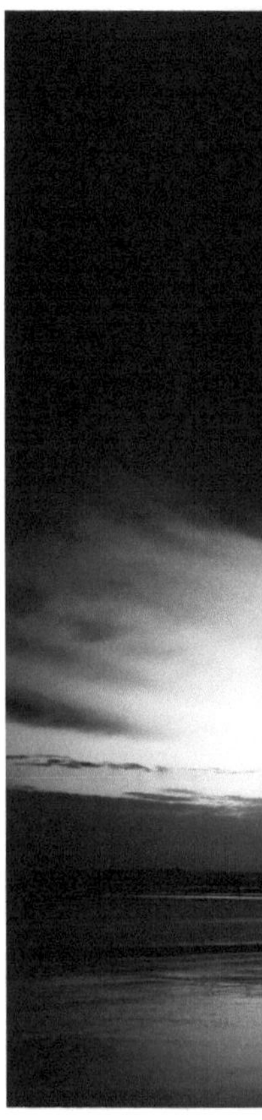

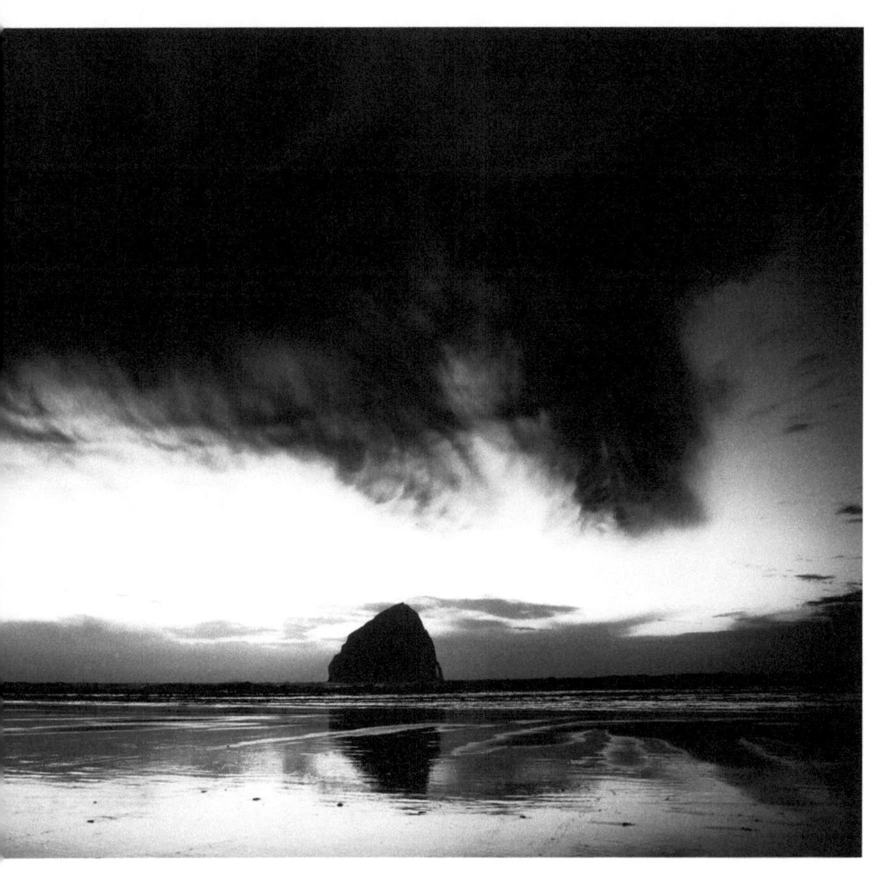

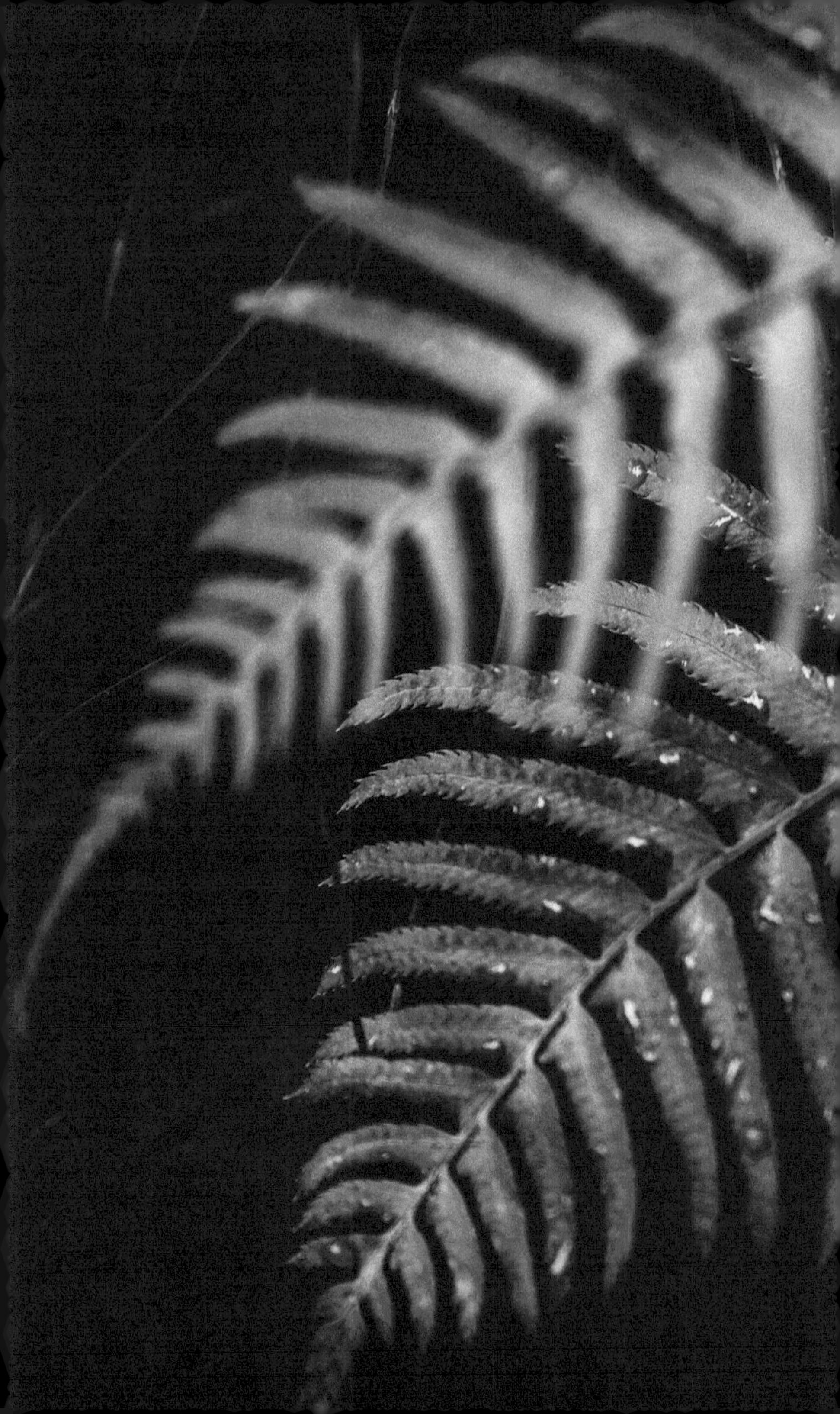

Make Two

Years of packing
Perfecting
The art of making
Larger things compact
Stores of grief
Compiled
Grasped and stronger
Until it could be
No longer held
in my skin
Seeping
Out of pores

Duplicate me
Make two
One to leave here
Free to love you
The way I have
always wanted to
Wished to

It will rain each day
I spend with you
Drops of water
Trickling down
Sword fern fronds

Space for oxygen
Between pinnules
Rest there
Counting my hours
on your time
She

She will stay here
Living out what was
Decided in service
Pushing at the pull
Action's reaction

Fixed
5.1 degrees relative
to the ecliptic.

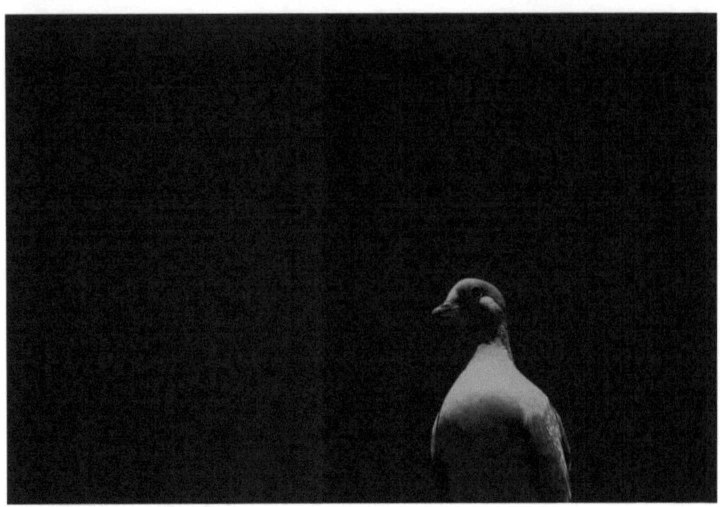

The Unraveling

The day they came for me
I did happen
to be calm
No rope in hand
in reach body
splayed basking
spread
Uncharacteristically
atop its armor
Warm to the touch

Call of the mourning dove
Angel
army heralding the unraveling
six substances of
grief blood/iron/steel/
wood/sisal/glass

Removal of cellular
Memory
Digging out
the pieces
Shards/strands
Splinters/
Congealed substances
My excavation

Site boundary
a line drawn between
My heart and the world
Space for what is mine
Room to breathe
Break
my own survival
Patterns to accept
That not everything
Can
be saved

And now
release
From earth bound
Duty
Discerning where
The grief ends
and I begin

Will I no longer cry
at the beauty
Pain of your absence
The space between gasped
breaths
Will disappear
Taking the color
Spectrum of (grief)
From my world

Will I no longer reach
For my pen
Relief from
The recurring floods
Cut out from
Lifeline to this world

Will you no longer feel
My grief
strings tugging always
Keeping your heart
Bound to mine

Will my eyes set
When the horizon
Seen from above
Diminish
the difference
Between day and night

Will it feel like failure
regret firm
ground not clouds
underfoot dust
settling
No echoes
When I call your name
Through the trees.

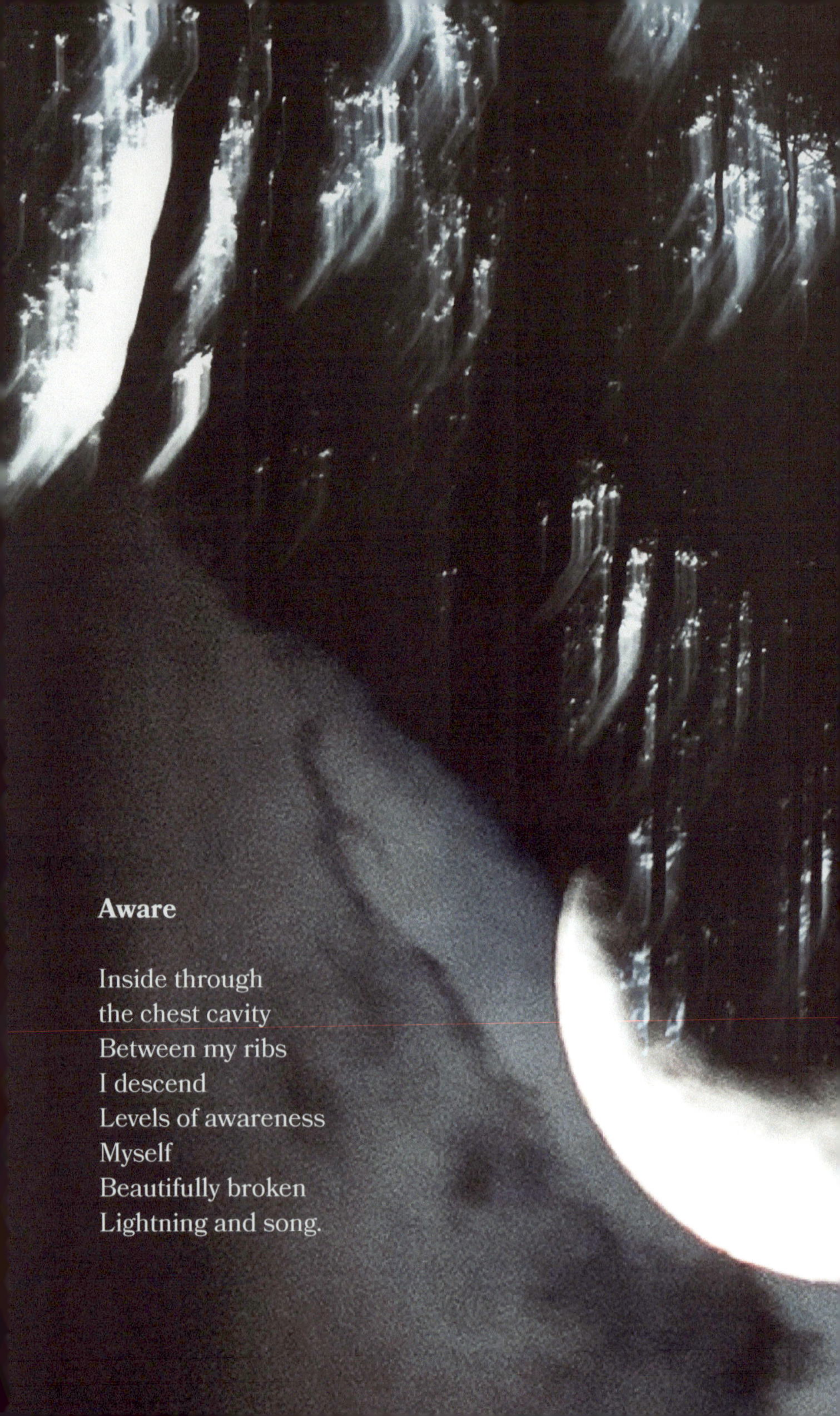
Aware

Inside through
the chest cavity
Between my ribs
I descend
Levels of awareness
Myself
Beautifully broken
Lightning and song.

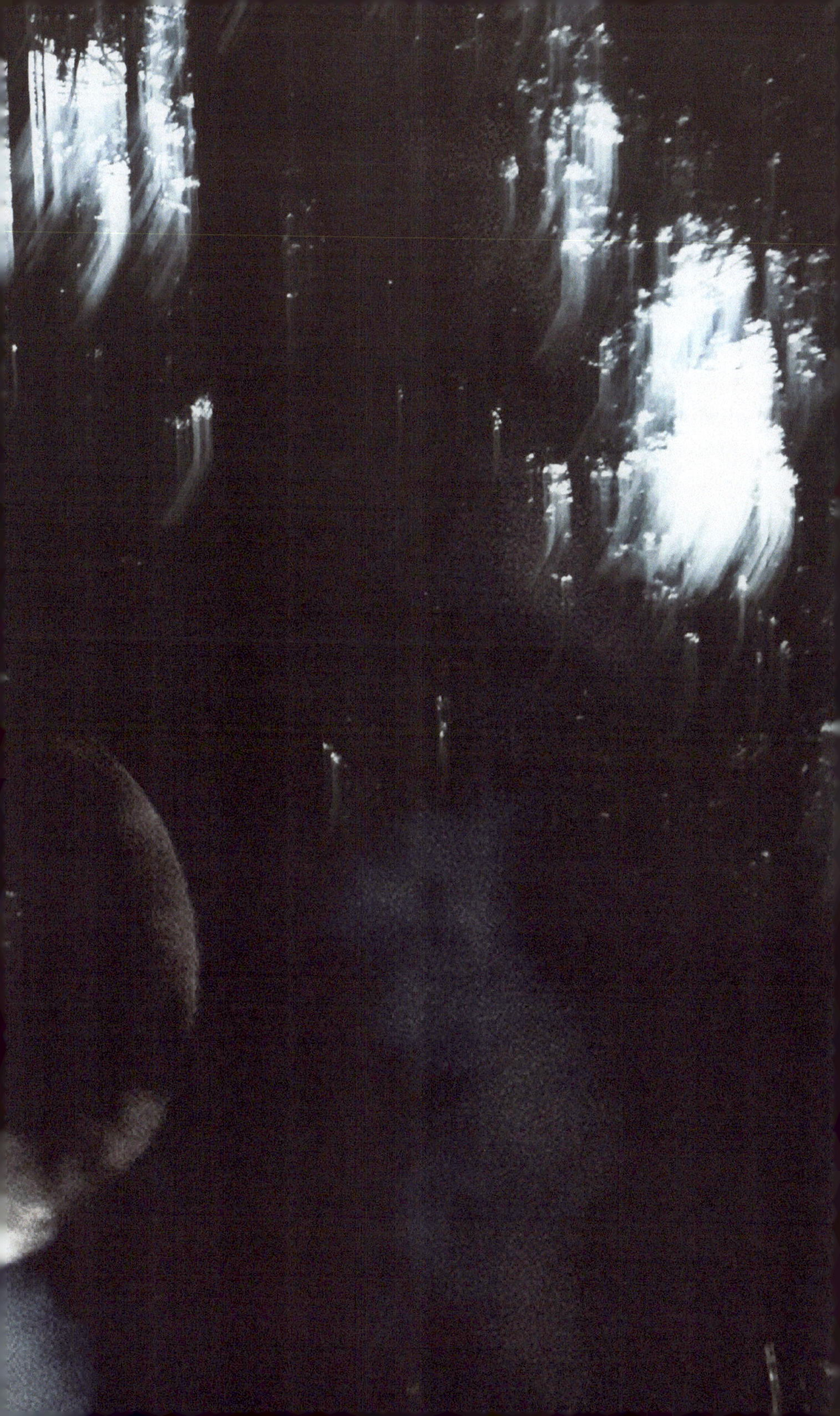

Faith

I count the days
Wonder
The moments
Do you think of me?
I know the answer
Was it the road
diverging or stumble
Or am I charting
new territory
What if
I'm breaking
the ground
Towards fulfillment
It could be my work
That must be done
It could be necessary
Did you think of that
Did you allow
I may be following
Or have I lost
The way
Faith faith
Please have faith in me
What if
What if I'm doing the work
I'm meant to do
To come back to you.

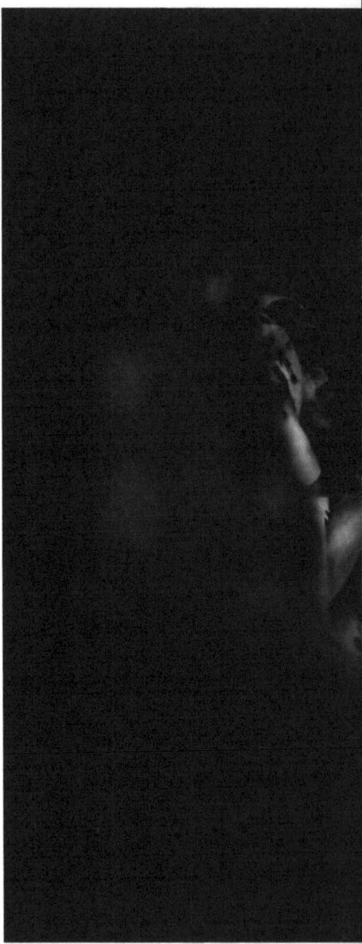

In Stillness

In stillness
Sifting and sorting through
Your absence
Grateful grateful grateful
It chants to me.

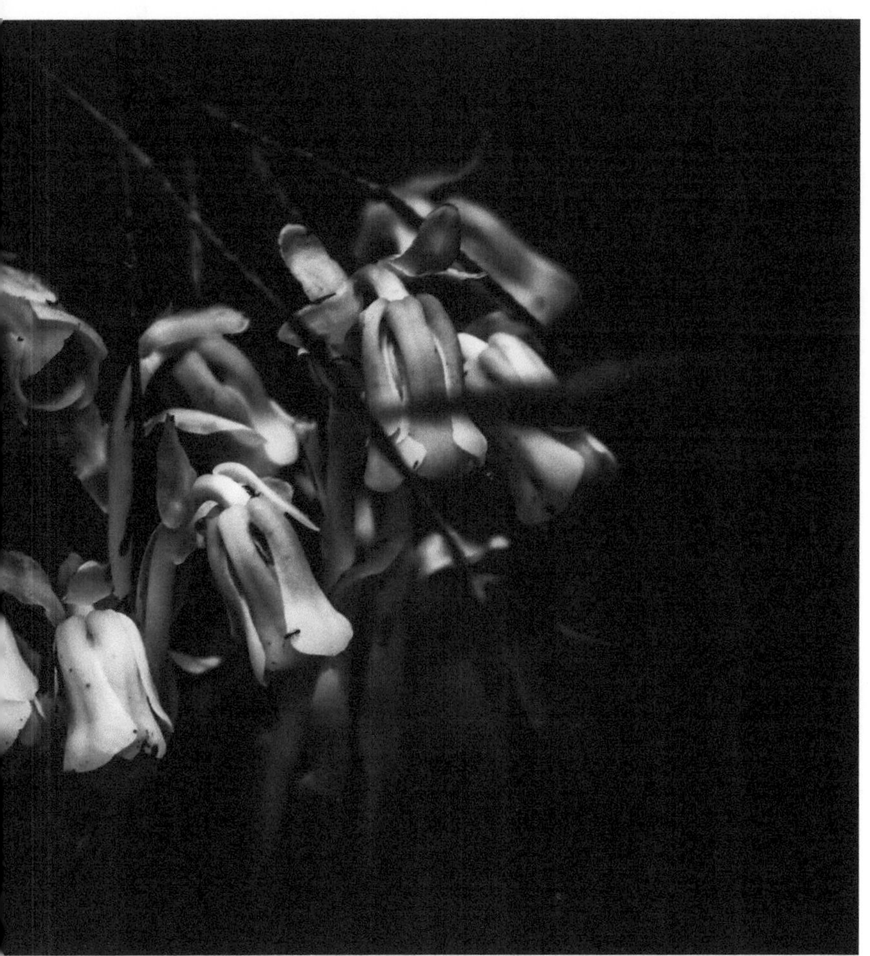

Graveyard

Tiny seed of doubt
Fear of abandonment
Am I
good enough
To live in this world?
I am
too good
To live
in this world
More powerful
than you know
She says
Forgotten power
What power is this?

I can already
destroy a dream
With a flick of my finger
Present you
your new reality
Welcome you to hell
With my smile
The light in my eyes
easy to follow
You won't notice
You are walking
through your own graveyard
Where all the ravens
Answer to me.

Tangled

That was my best
Farther
I didn't have
A vine watered
Cared and loved
Grown to take
My breath
Thorns
Stem encircling
strangling
Wild
Tangled in the garden
I should have left you.

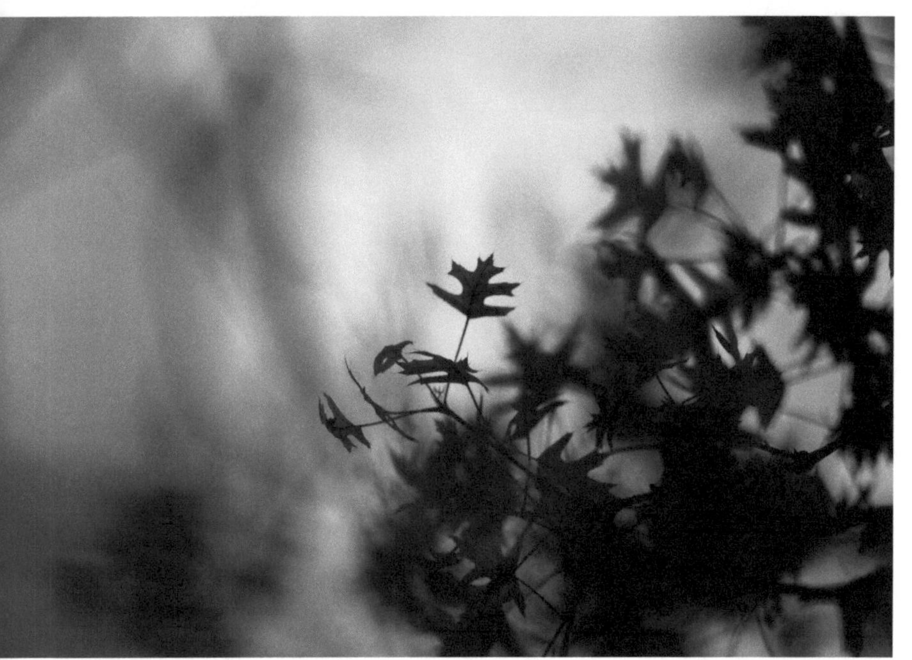

Waves

A list generated
Methods of hurt
Your specialties
I cross them off
As they occur
Having ridden your
Waves

Before my bones
are stronger
More difficult for you
To break
Approaching the crest
I gather the splints
Regardless

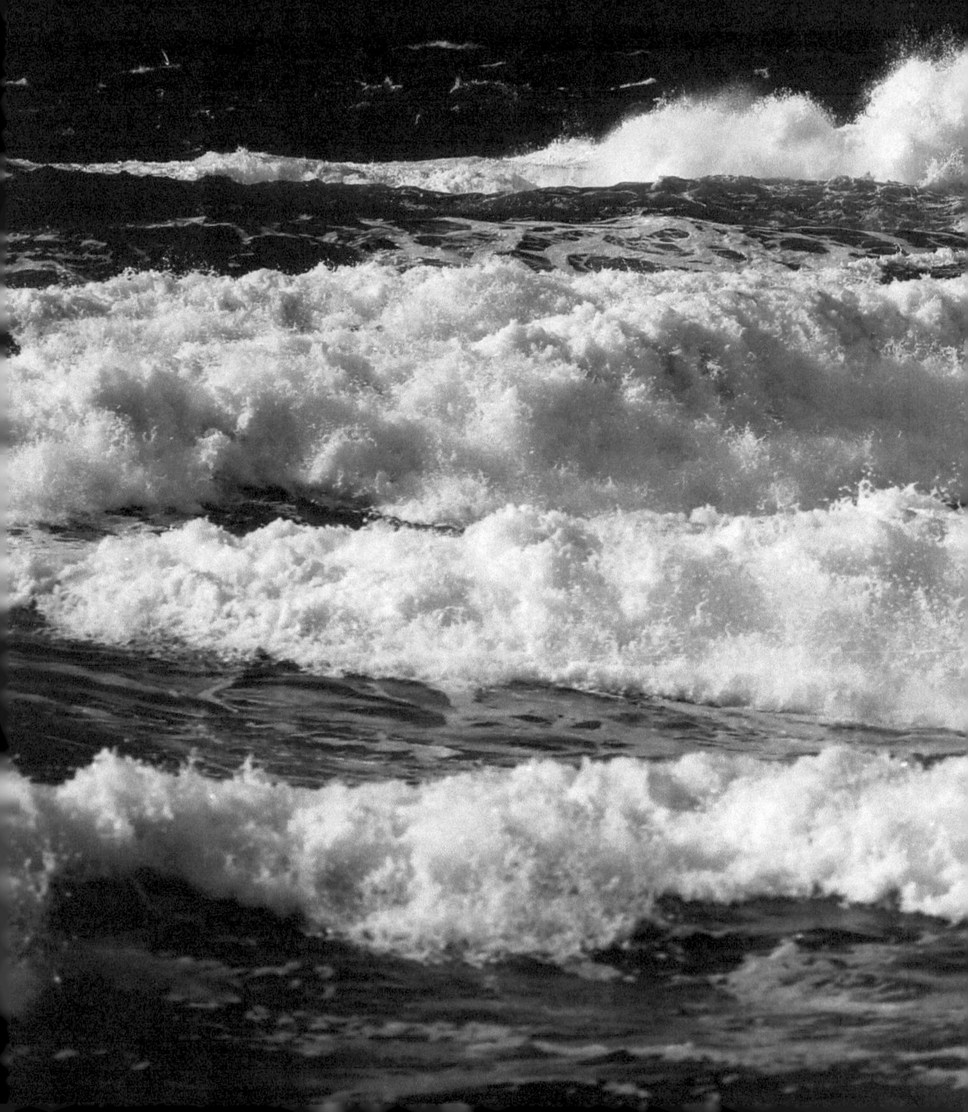

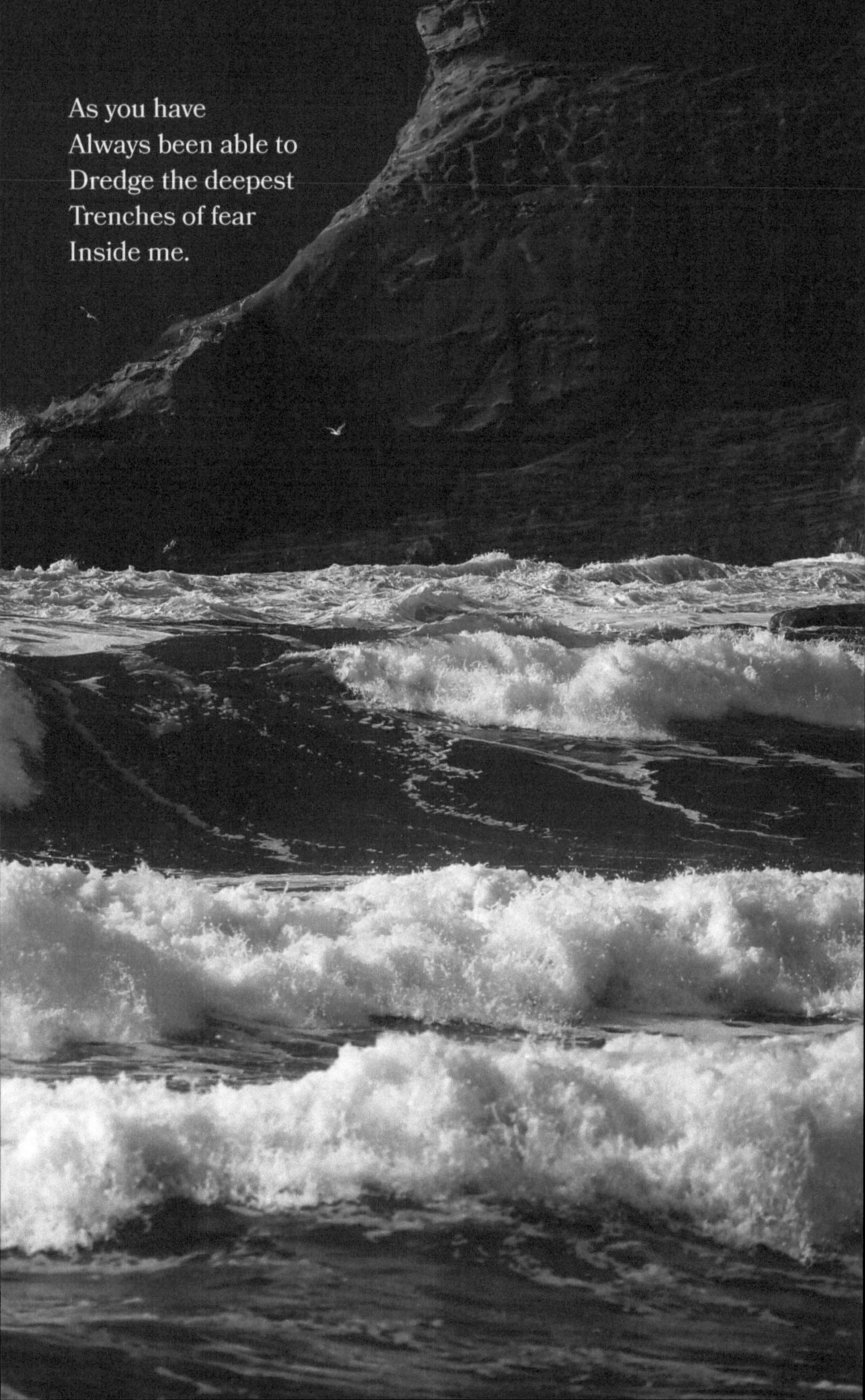
As you have
Always been able to
Dredge the deepest
Trenches of fear
Inside me.

How Did You

Where were you that day
What did you look at
To remember
How did you
Bring yourself
To breathe
in a presence empty
When wind lifted the branches
And you stopped to pause
Did your lips turn upward
in the semblance of a smile
Did you like
Yourself chewing
Feeding
Your disease.

Tide

My tide
your arms heavy
Push and pull
Your feet ever unsteady
Drag you the full length
Wax to wane.

Story

I tell myself
A different kind
of story
Similar shade
As I'm difficult to fool
So adjust starting point
Curve you slightly
To the left
Reduce your heart by half
at least
Eyes that see when shut
Press my finger to your lips
Lead you down a darkened
narrow hallway
Place you in a corner
Where I can't.

What is Left

When I strip away
The lies
Peel them off
Your skin
Protective covering
Put on as
And now
The dead
Decayed flesh
Found underneath
Eaten away
No longer you
Or the true you
What is left
Love.

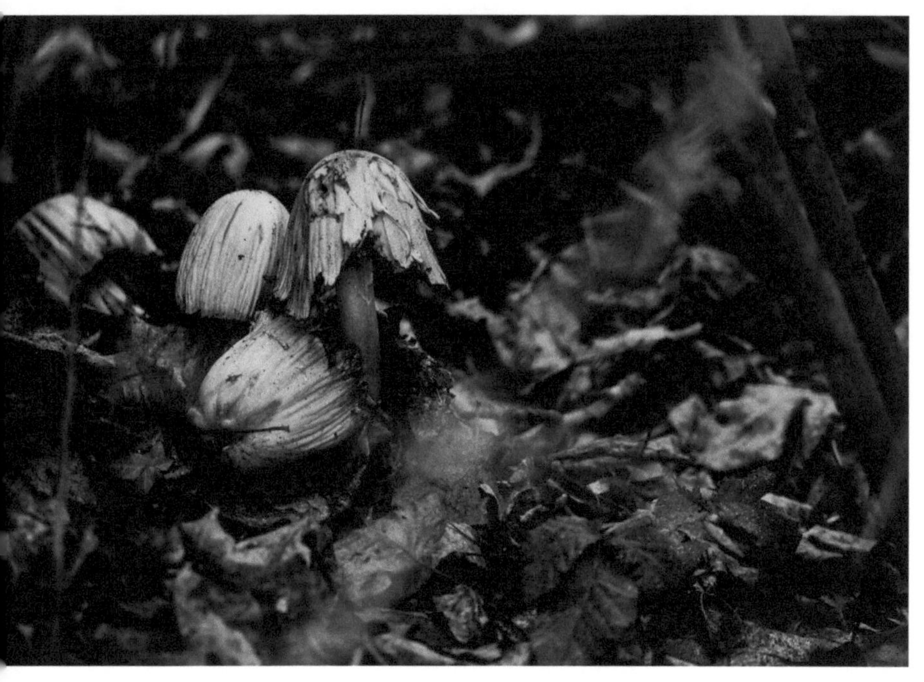

No Way Out But Through

Confused
Four corners
To an empty sky
You call
Powerless
Flying in circles
Hearing the rumblings
From underground
Your taproot
Calling you to source
No difference
All choices
Ending at the beginning.

Among the Waste

Dirt is difficult to unlearn
It is warm under the soil
Among the roots
Among the waste
Revel there once
You may become
Necessary few
among your kind
Are found such
successful decomposers

Other uses for white wings
Underground
Feather fodder
It is a strange thing to see a great bird
Cradling centipedes
Instead of feasting upon them
Despite gifts
eventually merging
only where we lay

It is not lonely
Below the surface
Company compounds
The more flesh
The more friends
you will find
Hungry and
The sky is far to go.

Unable to Swim

Ending
Walking away
From the one thing choking
Drowning in its depths
Unable to swim
In one inch of water
too fearful to stand
Leave it
facedown in the mud
Covered in disease
Tended by the salt
Tongue licking
Rawness
body sagging
Flesh loose and hanging
from rotting joints
Gills will return
It will learn to breathe
again
Beginning.

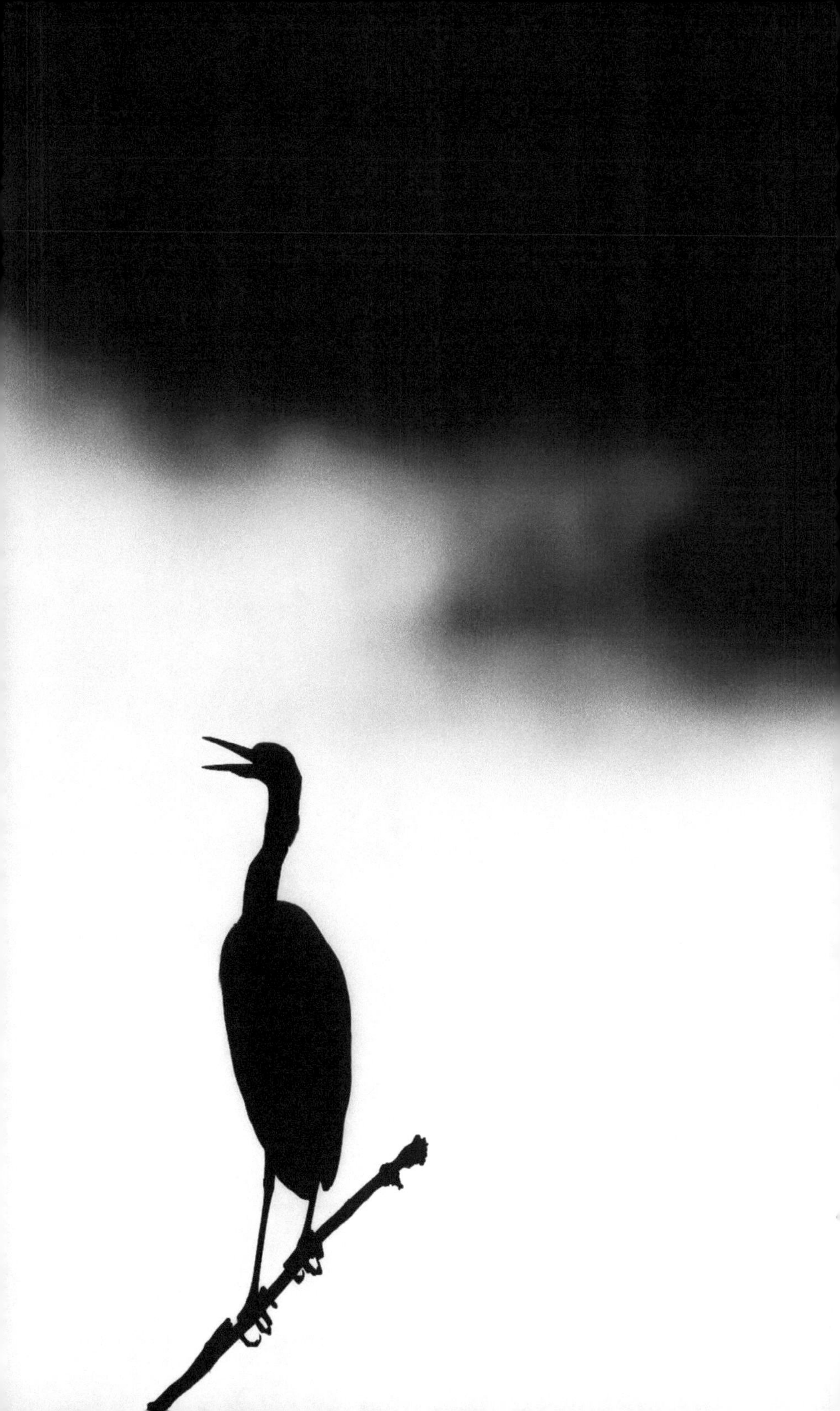

Fool's Errand

I was only required
To save you once
To take the long road
Home
To the beginning
Follow it to a grave
Where you paced
Awaiting decree
Your birthing

I walked where
and ran
Through light
and shadow
Picking boughs of
Pine to lay lightly
At your feet

I laugh as I kneel
Your disbelief
Your rise and fall
Watching me
Snake
Through the eye
of the needle

The gifts of truth
You wished for
Arrive whole
The unlauded
Power
of vulnerability

To love the moon
is surely
A fool's errand.

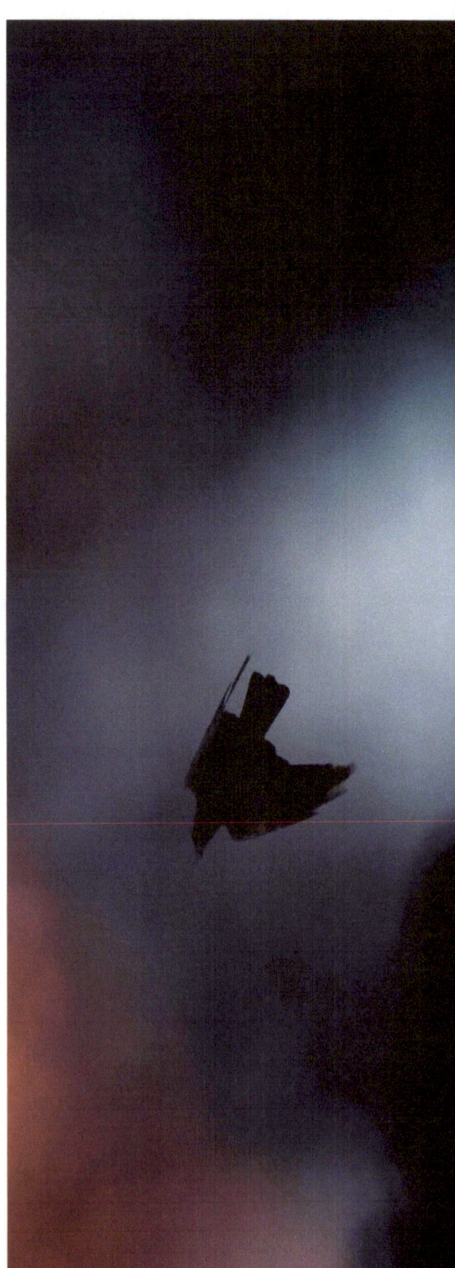

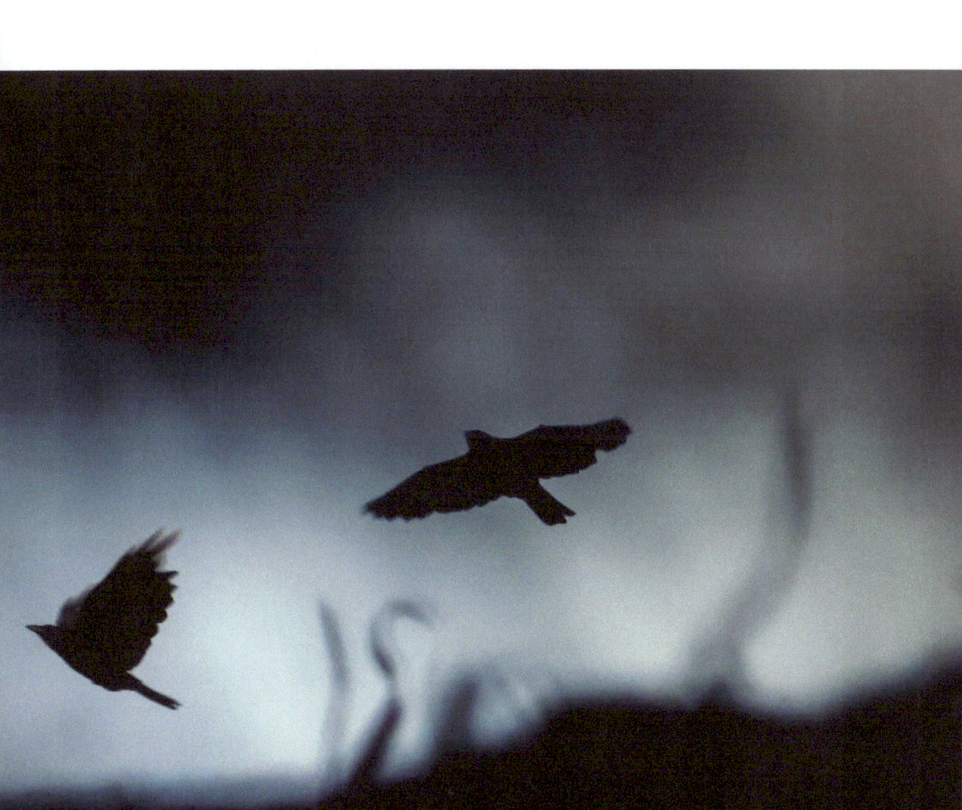

The Future

This card shows you the future outcome of the situation, given the current circumstances as they are, if the querent stays on their current path.

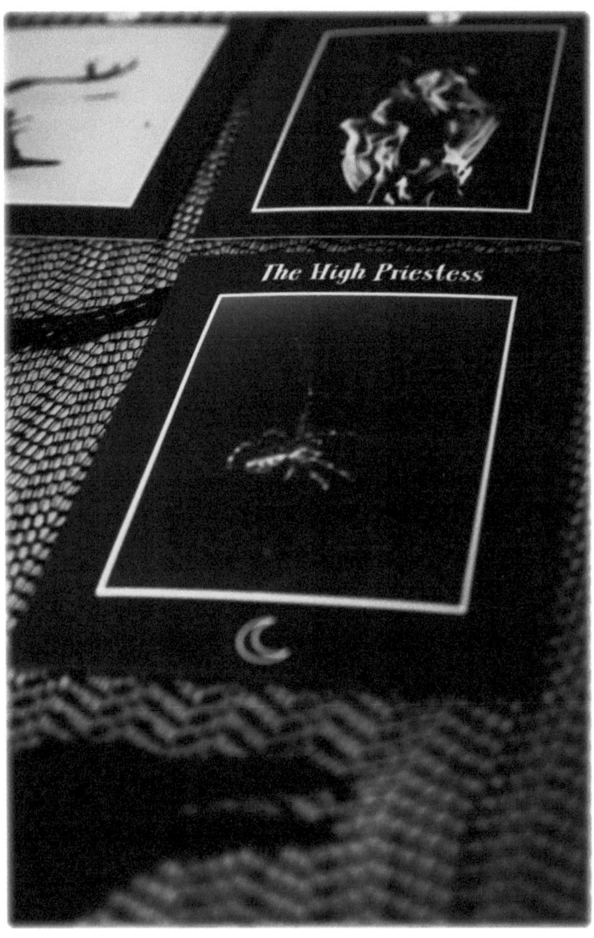

The High Priestess

the divine feminine

listen to your intuition

open to your spirituality

cooperate with spirit

let what is hidden come to the surface

search within yourself for the answers you seek

be patient with yourself, trust yourself

time of reflecting and retreating

from the world around you

look toward what is uncomfortable,

confront your fears

harmony between the rational and intuitive mind

Self-Fortification

Weight
Not a burden but
Giving rise
to a downward force
On celestial craters
Rilles and mountains
Atomic weight
Relative to mass
Flightless
Sky resident
And so gathered
or it was given
The moon does dream
She dreams of a bird
bird or angel
Visibility sharpens
Down on the ground
Soft things
in hand
Branches to alight on
And rest
A guide
To self-fortification.

Retribution

Full moon
Fire spell
Expulsion of your
Poison heavy
Upright she stands
The time has come
as it ultimately does
For retribution
Unhappily she will hand
back the blade let
You make your own
Cuts

The daily spread of
Salt upon
Unholy wounds
Now
Your concern
Yours and those
Whose eyes were
Granted
Through deliverance
Fake form
Forming
Caricatures
Full access
of the remains.

Penitence

Let myself remember
When my gaze
Turned upward
Before
Your binding
Learned hands
To myself
To you

When windows
Precaution
were opened
So the neighbors
or birds
Could hear any screams
Issuing
Under learned hands

Drag me
Drag me
Drag me
Still you could
never quite
take me
Under
Never me
Knocking
on your door

If I rub salt
Rosemary oil
Holy water
dispersed
Through the walls
The floor
Will it clean
Memories
me too.

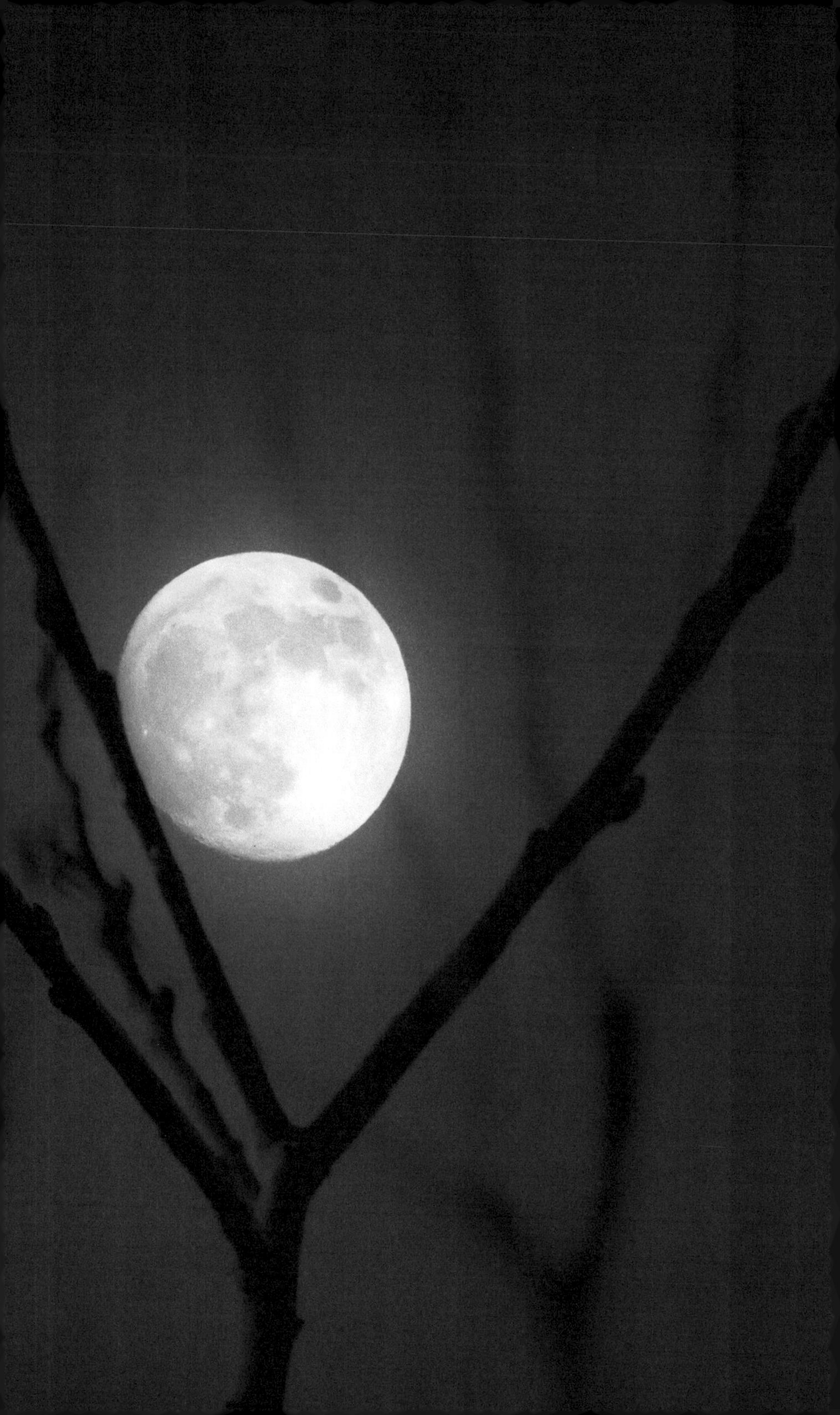

Finally

Finally
I have decided
to move aside
No longer
Stand
Between you
and the fear

My back is bruised
tongue a dagger
Prices of your protection
Depth of craters

Cry forsaken
Doesn't matter what I do
At this point
It is coming
For you
Payment in
Pieces
of you claimed

There will be
No soft curve
for tucking blame
No reflected light
Illuminating your way.

Oneness

Whatever made me
Believe
I could be anything
But fragmented
More than a phase

You think your
Onlyness
Oneness
Will save you
Make me
Give in
No

Your gifts
I shall take
and go.

Hands

Hands I think
I no longer want to
Touch me
As they don't
Know me
What I've become

Hands that are now
An abyss
that I fear
The black space where
I can
No longer
Crawl into you.

Unseen

Denial suggests you
don't know if
you are lying
Reaching
Come to the other side
Walk with me
a field blooming
Still relevant
in darkness
I can grow
You can't be angry
Blossom
Still count
Still love
Unseen.

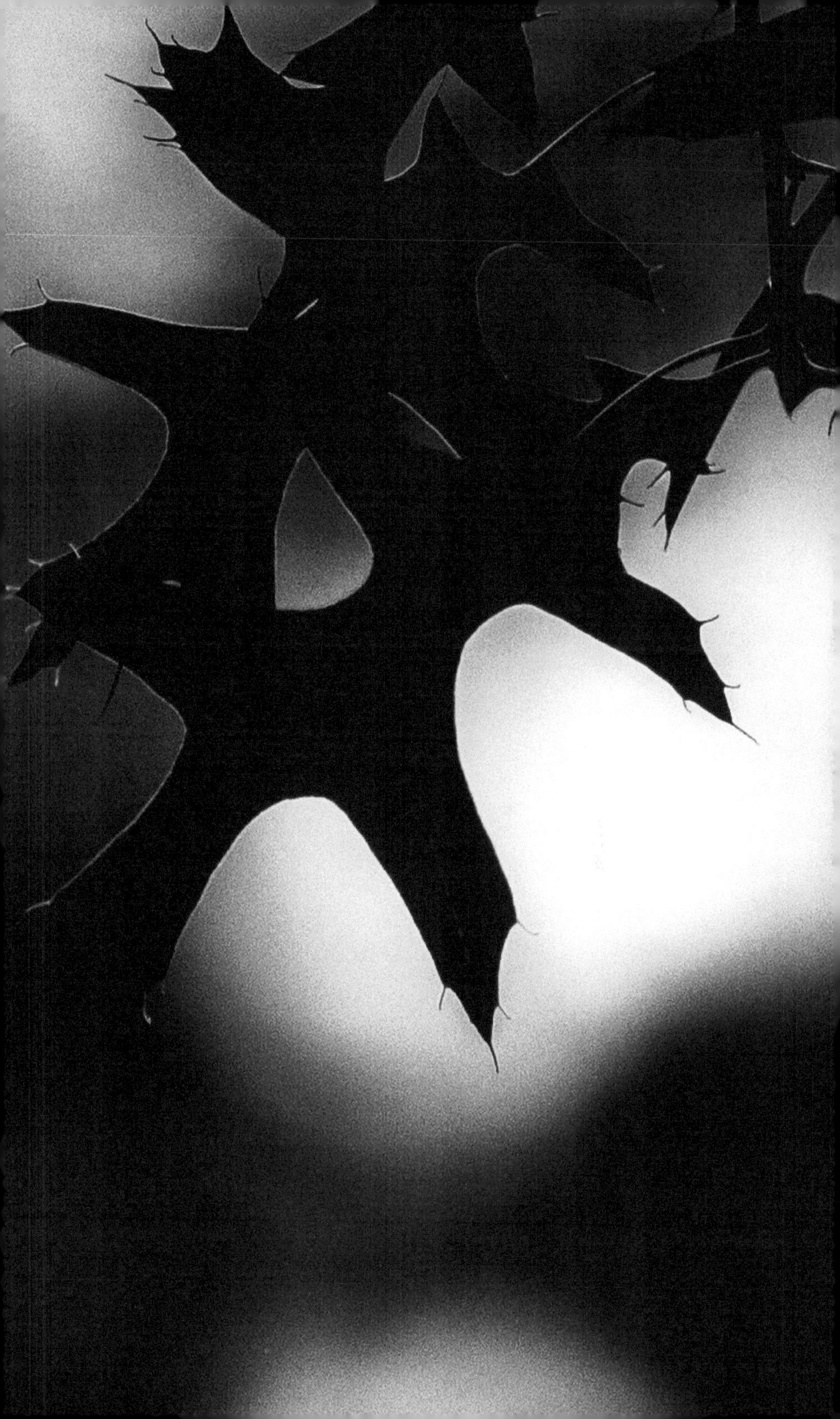

Medicine

I will learn
To touch myself
Softly again
Tell my body
I am sorry
I should have done
better convince her
Promise only
Not require her
To be someone else's
medicine.

You Think You Can

You think you can
Pick that memory up
Whenever you choose
Lick it clean
again
Taste me
When I'm not
Near you

I journeyed miles
the rounded curve
Beneath the surface
the long travel down
to transparency
And found what I left
At the beginning

I did not save you
Only to have to then
save myself
From you.

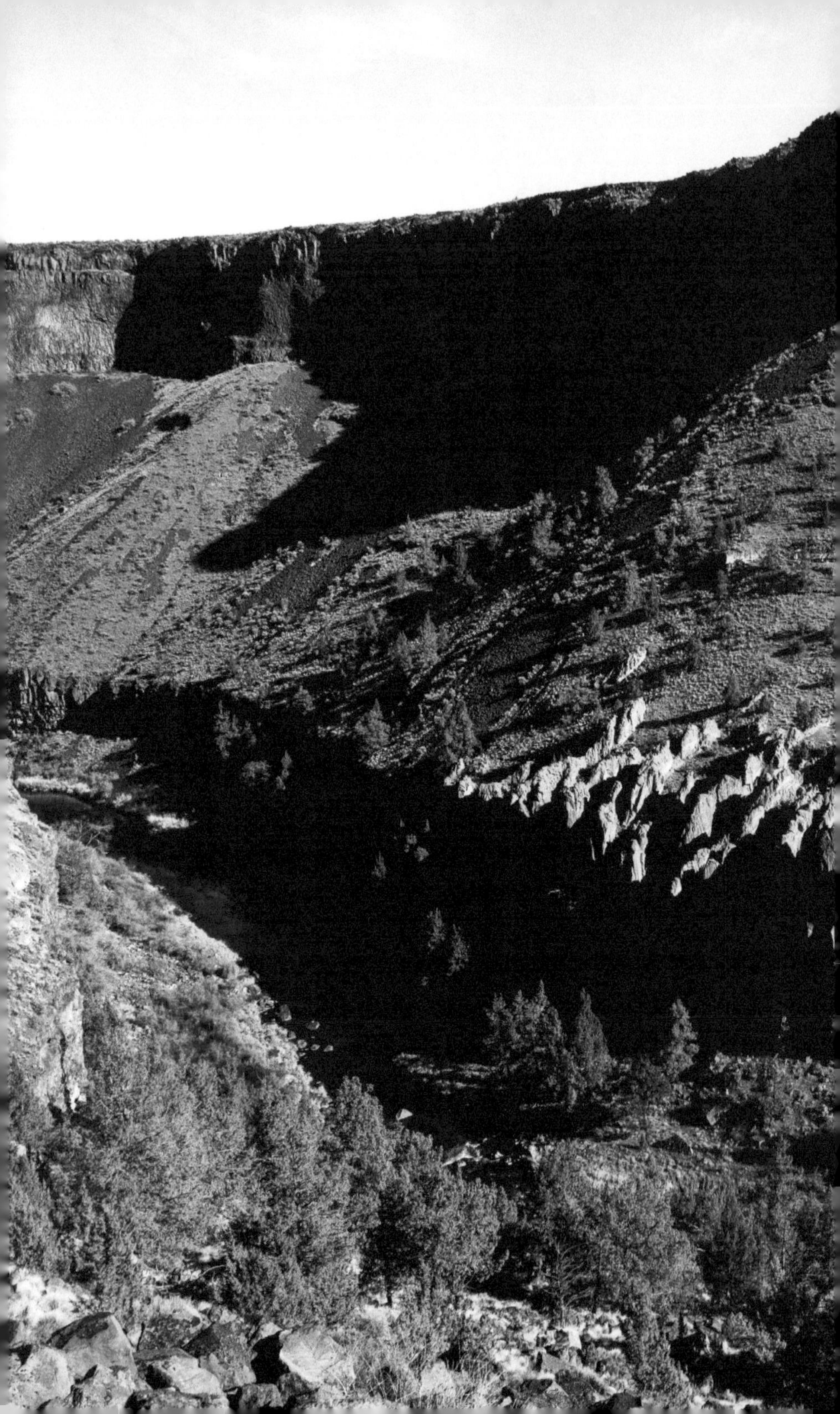

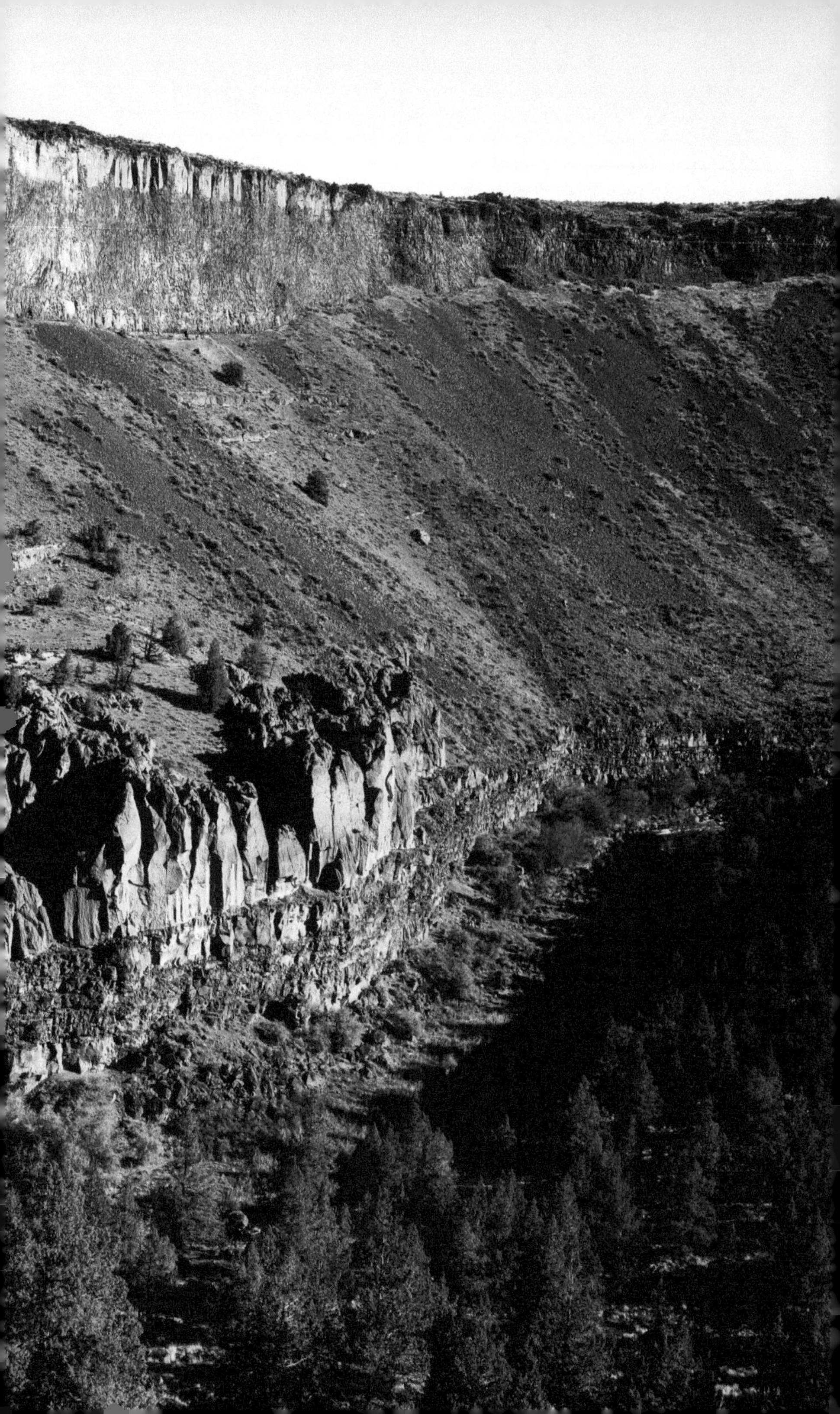

Thirsty

The windswept canyon
Thirsty
For the river
that once
Cut through
Shaping it
Crests of white surf
Carved borders
newly defined curves.

Instigator

Mode of travel
Shove down
Kick down tossed
Hurtle
In the middle of the curve
Under
I rest
Listen   feel   be
Know
And back up   I must go

And then spending time
Searching for someone who
Can take me down again
Dependent on brute force
Causation   reaction
To the black place

What if I want
To learn
To take myself
Lone traveler
Down my own road
Melting
Particles reshaping
By my own
Moonlit
Power
What use
Then
Do I have of you
Instigator.

Walk Away

If you can
Walk
Away go
It won't matter
Because
Then you were never
Who I thought you were
Anyway and
I no longer have to
Believe
In you, love.

Let Go of Your Story

I could finally claim
Wholeness
And because
You cannot
Smash me to pieces
Again
Human vulnerability
Should not be
A weapon
Worthy of a true
Warrior
Your knife blade
My teacher
Your false
Renouncement of
Love
My absolution
Your wish to
Continue inflicting
Pain and punishment
Mountains only
Faith
can move.

No Alternatives, No Solutions

Your high priestess
contemplates faithful
Motionless having
Completed
her web of fate
Each strand of silk
A divine lesson
for your learning
Straining
To free yourself
You create your own
Prison
Ultimately
you knew and
What better way to go
Her lambent eyes
No alternatives
No solutions.

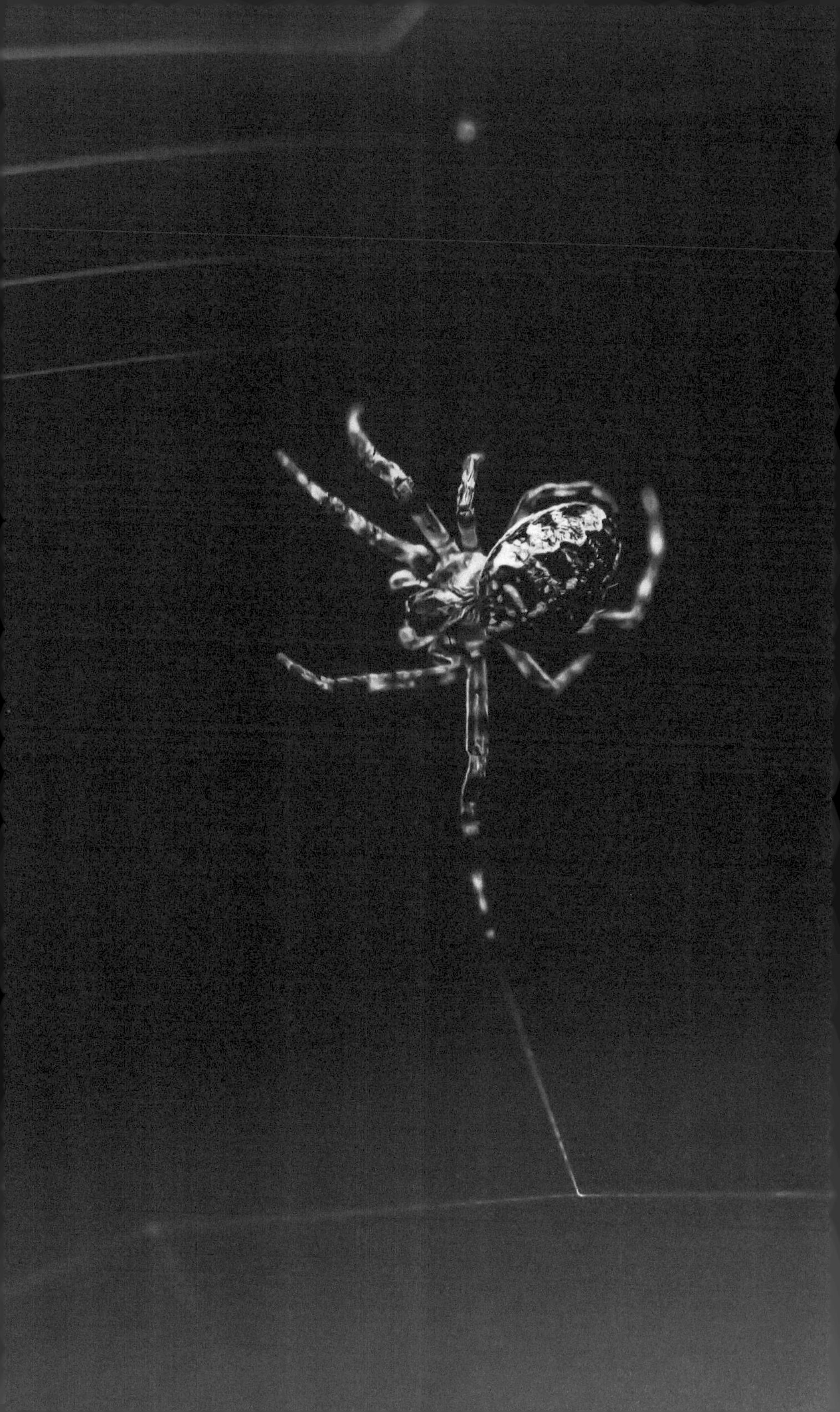

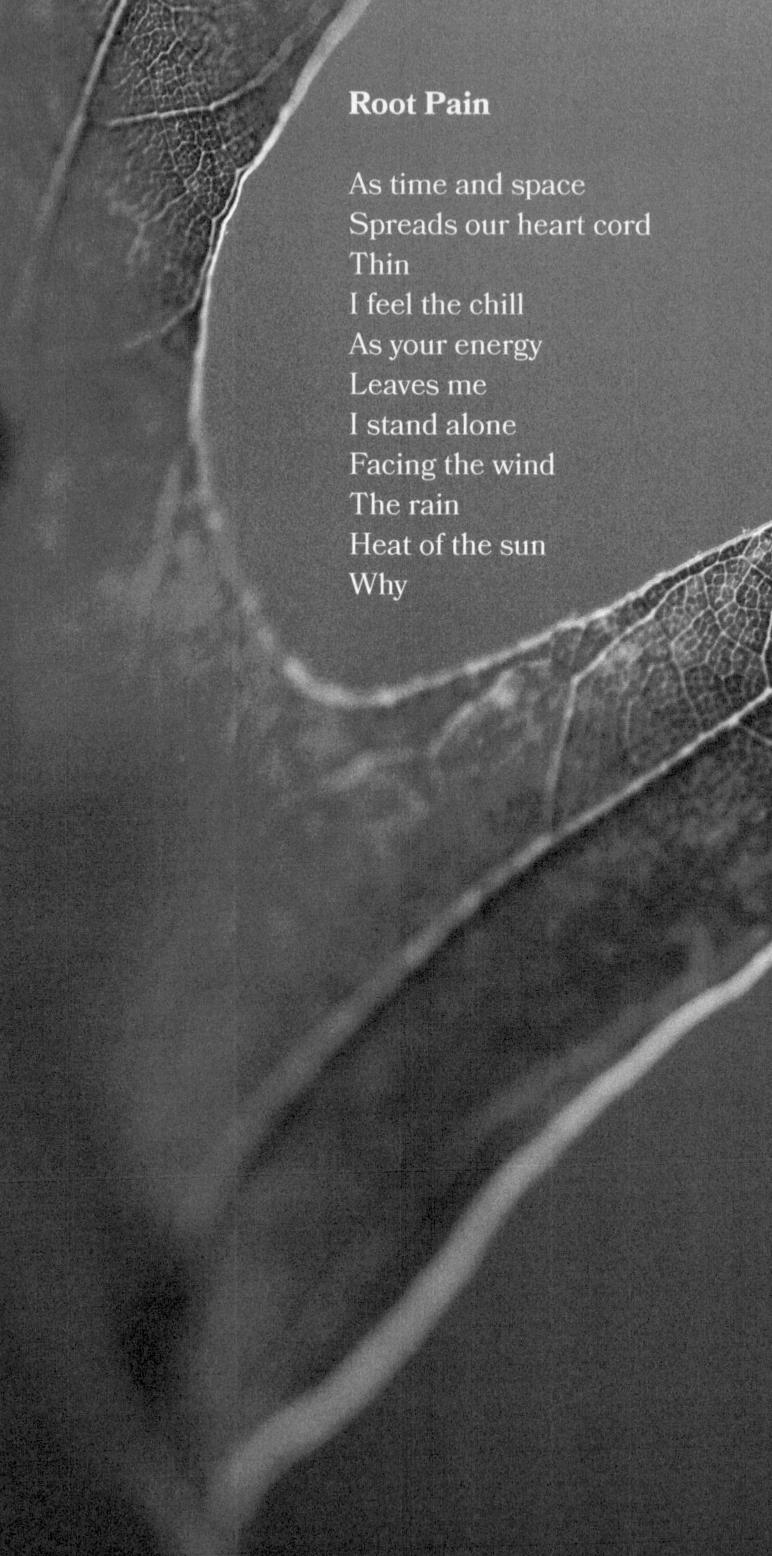

Root Pain

As time and space
Spreads our heart cord
Thin
I feel the chill
As your energy
Leaves me
I stand alone
Facing the wind
The rain
Heat of the sun
Why

To honor myself
How could you
Force me
To choose this

If you
Love me
You would
Love yourself first
Instead striking
Placing the knife where
A bloom should be
I cut you
For you
Why
Do you require
Unconditional love
Without delivering

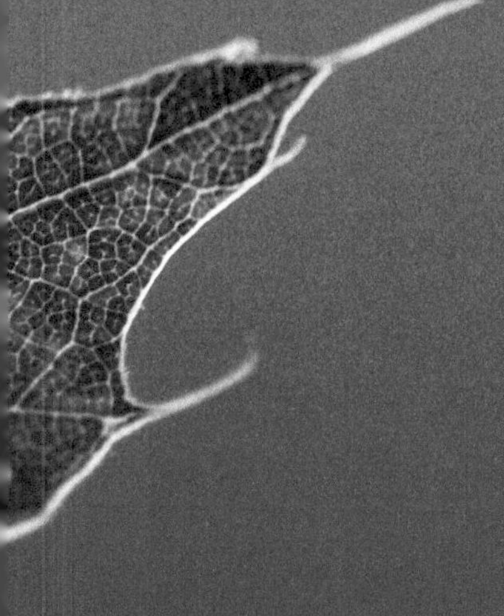

My root system
Stretches far beyond
I don't remember
Agreeing to stay
Without
Please stop please
stop please stop
Kneel for
My heart can't bear
this.

See Me

Inserting
Your hatred
Sorrow
Over your mother and
Mother of your children
Into me
The only woman
Who has ever loved
Cared for you
Desecrate your
Safe space
Fling blame
Accusations
The women
You wish to
Punish
Don't reside
in this
Flesh.

Don't Look Away

In the shadow
Healing
Intention
A promise to
Not hold
the pain
A promise to
Not need
the pain
To keep me
Steady
I won't need
a wound
Reminder
To say no
Don't
Look away.

Roots

The goddess in the tower
Becomes the tower
Itself
grows roots
Shattering
itself inside out
freedom
Room to breathe

Broken stone fragments
Once her skin
Hardened
Chiseled in defense
Protecting
The true weapon
Love
Buried within

Downstairs are calls
shouts cries
No time to look out
As she unpacks the marvel
of herself

Her new skin
Breathing
Breathing and alive
Vulnerable, exposed
and yet
Home.

Third Pillar

Reward the rights
Strength to hold
My breath
Bilateral
Rising and falling
in accordance
with the sky
Forever seated
The bearer tasked
Guardian of the gateway
The third pillar
the only entrance
To the path
between.

Soul Essence

I watched
you jump
Right over
The edge
My edge
You just turned
Away from me
Ran to it
Gave me one
Last look
and jumped

I hear
your screams
From afar
and I do
Dream
of following
You I love so
Yet here
I stay
Rooted
Soaking up
Your soul
Essence like
Water vapor.

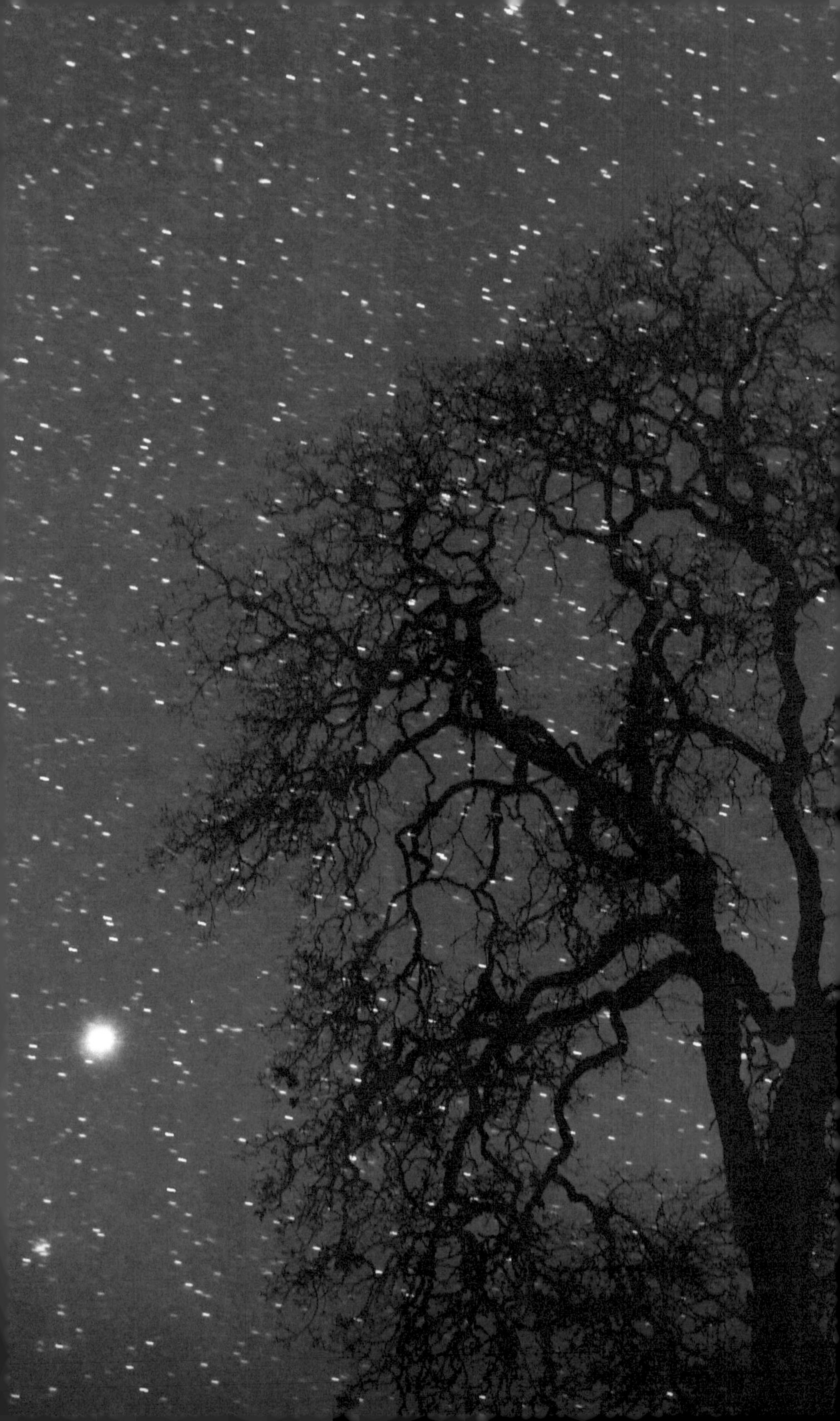

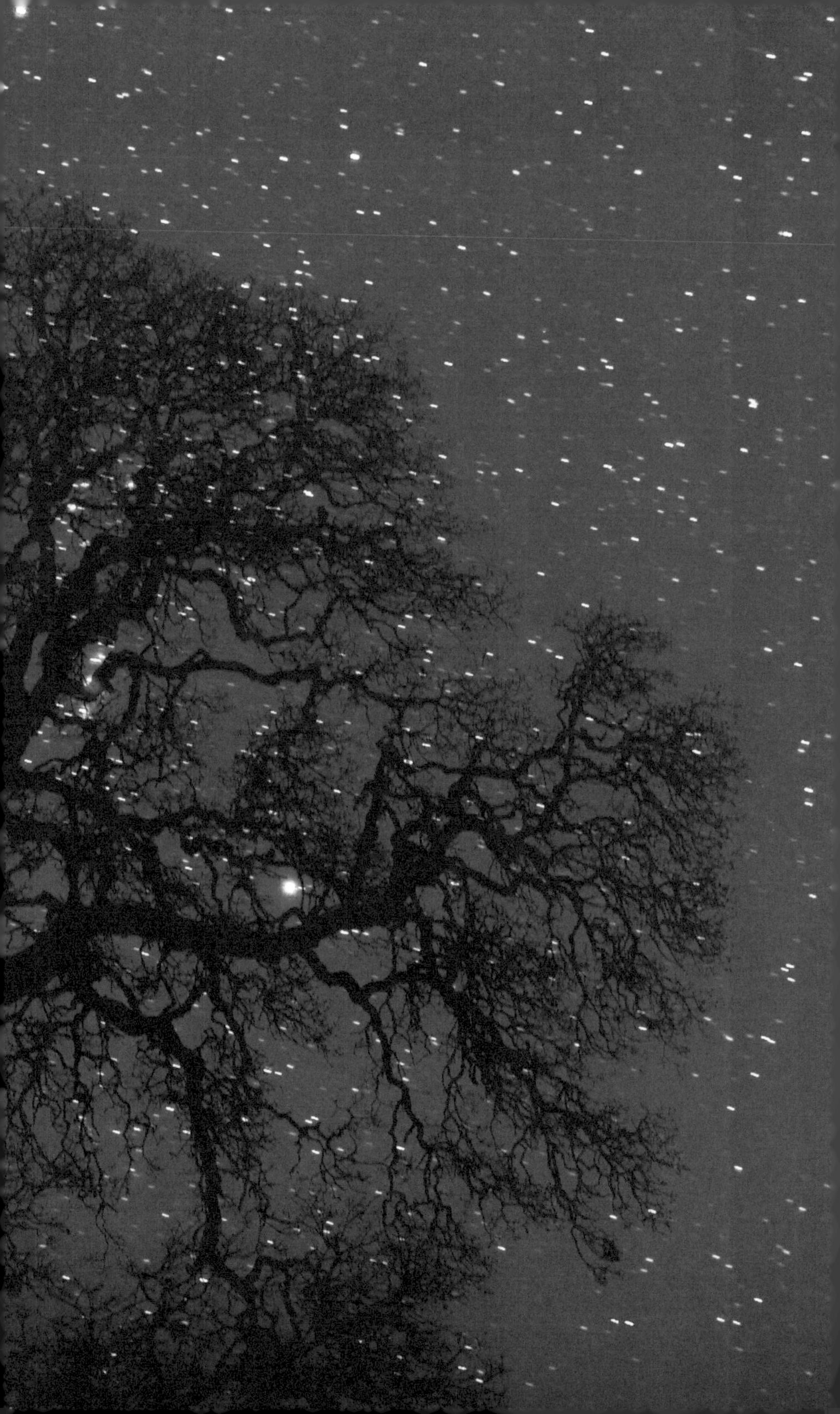

In Gratitude

Thank you
For insistence
Opening
my windows
to let in
All the light
Air
And sounds
for my right
To worship mine
helping me
Release
all I fear
My shadow self
empowering me
To be fully
She

I will not
hate you
for running
Once you saw
What you had done
I too once feared
All of this
Beauty and terror
Duality
As all pure things
Exposed

I will not
blame you
For abandonment
As I am happy
to be left
Alone
with this
Myself
Holding all phases
With equal regard

I will not shame
Your false
flight to safety
As you now face
a worse beast
Alone
Seemingly unfit
As you have chosen

Maybe someday
I will see you
And him
together
in harmony
Such as me and mine
Or perhaps I will simply
Hear rumors of the tale
Merge attempt
the destruction
Such sealing
your fate
Either way
in gratitude, my love.

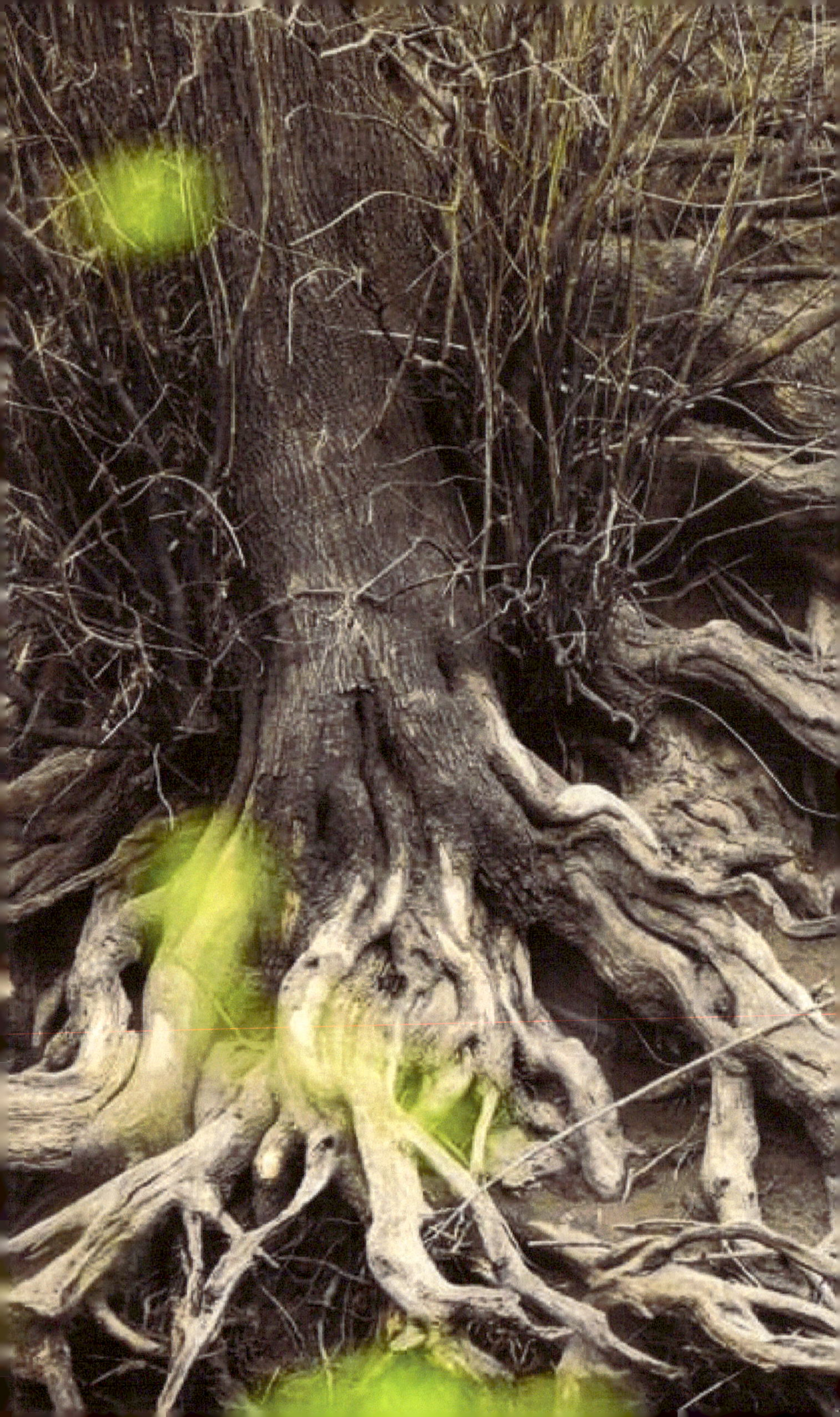

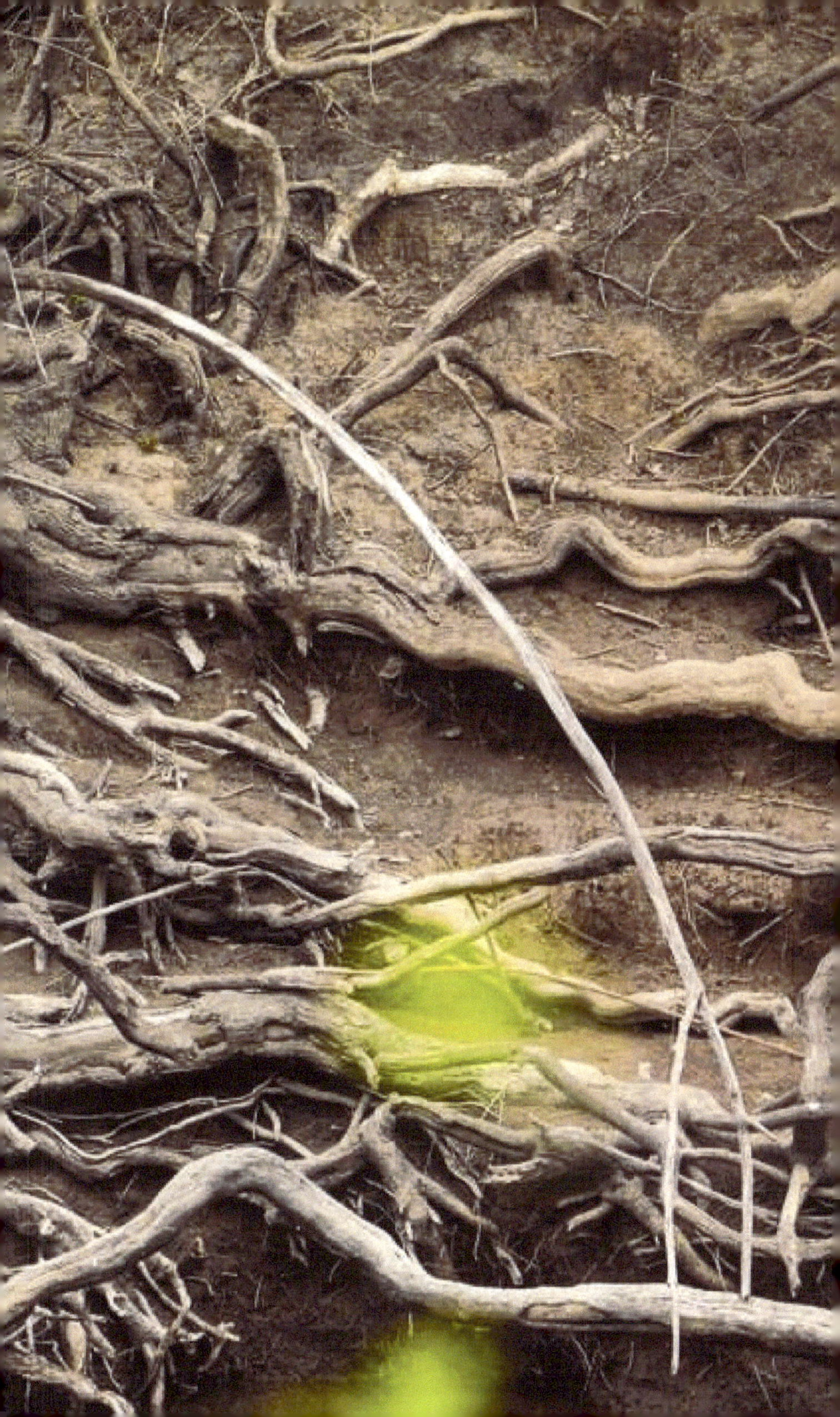

Potential

*This card reveals the possible outcome
that can occur if the querent chooses to
take the advice given by cards 2 and 3.*

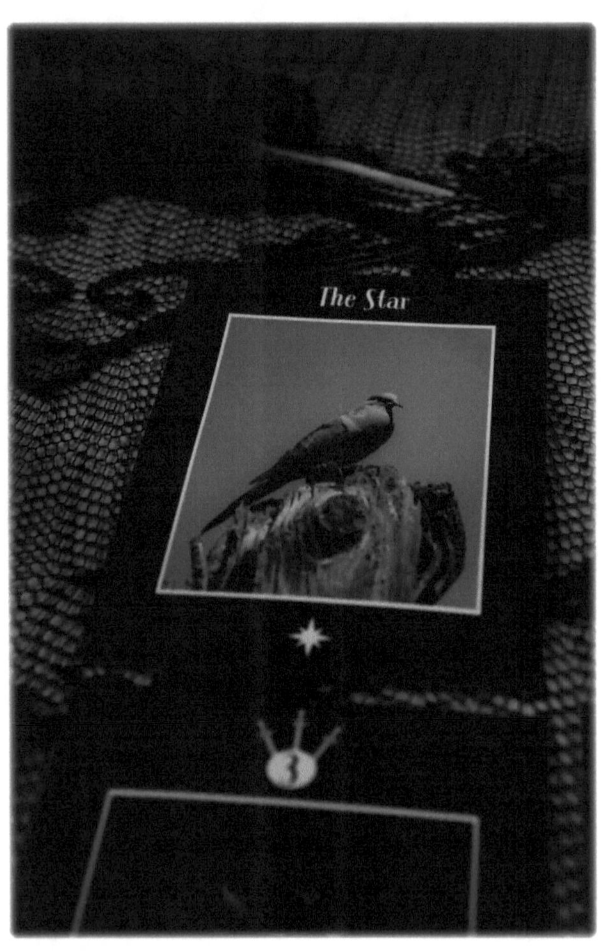

The Star

you passed through a terrible

challenge without losing hope

your loss helped you recognize your

own resilience and power

healing, you have navigated home to yourself

blessed by the universe

things are about to get better

embrace gratitude

nothing in the universe is ever truly lost

be true to yourself, listen to your intuition

whatever has changed, the essence remains,

strong and bright, burning within

Vernal Equinox

Vernal equinox
Birthplace of fire
And resilience
Shadows
lengthen exact
visibility is deceiving
I know you know
what lies beyond

Loud calls of geese
wild overhead

The migration
as the Earth tilts
unhinged
refusing to abide
The winds
like a pendulum
You swing.

Spring Thaw

A frozen river
Water only
Abundant in
Spring thaw
Now
As the sky warms
You can see the full
Contour
My lips
How they
Tremble awakening
Things inside you
Better left
Dreaming.

Bloom Worthy

What is a better word
For disappointment
Something to describe
the containment
holding
An expectation
Unfulfilled

What do I know
Only
Springtime flowers
are as beautiful
as the evergreen
or more
that you wished for

Was it for love
Hating
yourself understanding
Or for anger
Overriding
the frailty
or more
If I could be
You don't believe
a bloom worthy
Would I be
more to you.

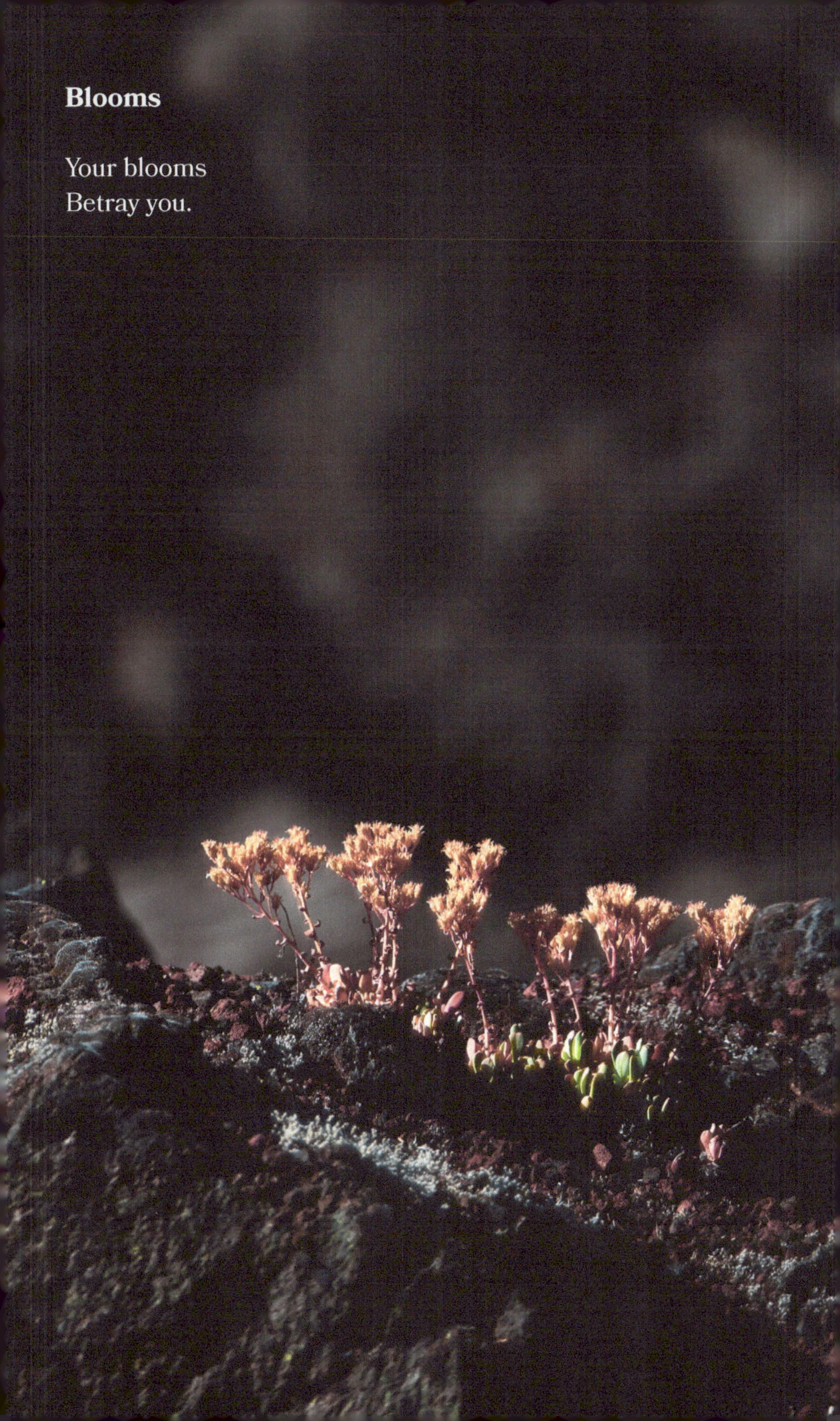

Blooms

Your blooms
Betray you.

Cleanse the Bones

The sky calling
Hope
to me
I find a place
under a cloud
Lick my wounds
Remember
What it felt like
To love him
Leave him
A red sunset
Pain
Coloring the twilight
Before the darkness
Watches him
Peel
the flesh from
His own bones.

Forgive

How many times
Do I have to
Forgive you
Before
You are able to
Forgive yourself.

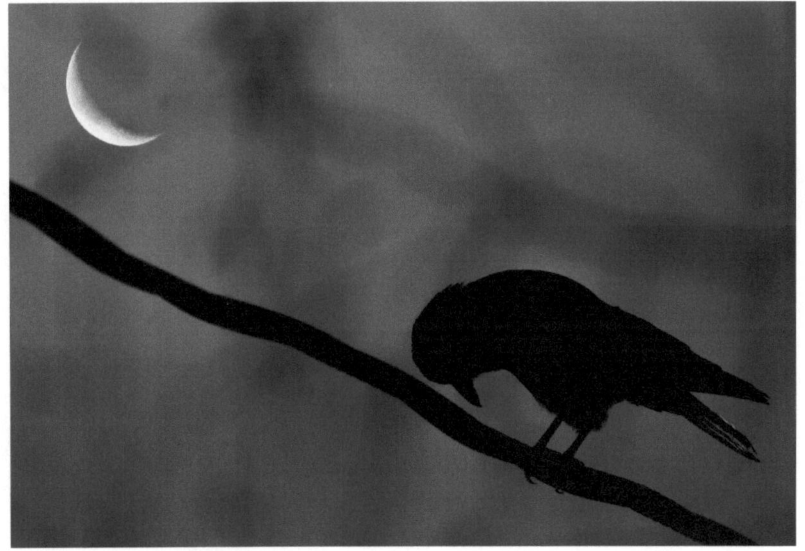

Lower the Frequency

Lower the frequency
Perhaps merely
Your angle
Less than
45 degrees of arc
You can close
a wound
No longer serving
a purpose
A remembered difficulty
An excuse for future hesitation
the waning
How if only
Would you
As I'm falling away
Soothe me.

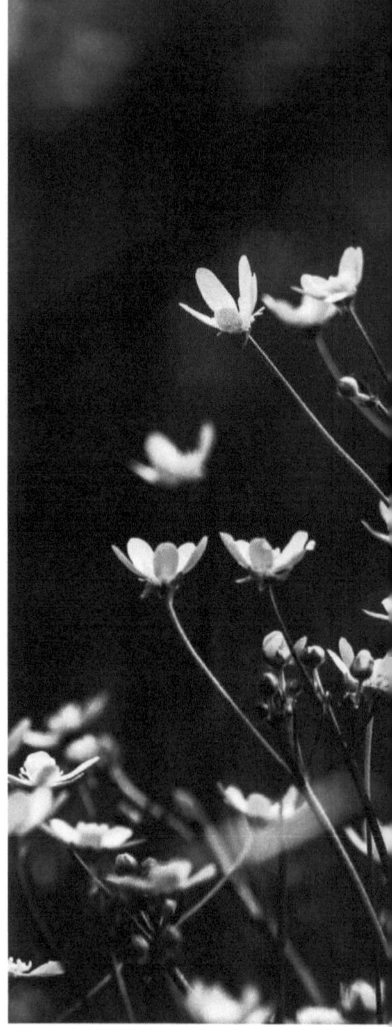

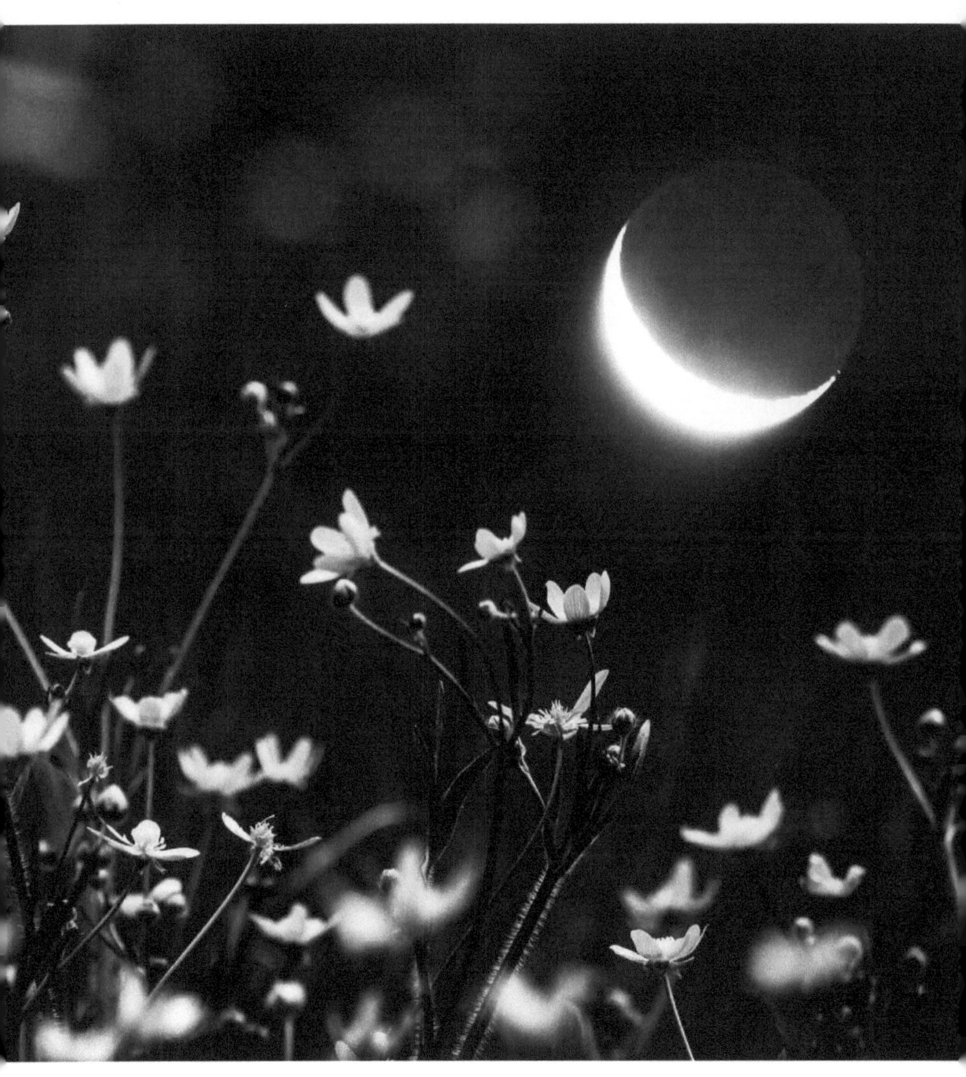

Waning

Fourteen days of waning
An accommodating
Amount of hours
Between now and new
The last cycle
involving any
Component of you
Each day I release
I let more go
Spaces within me
Open and free
Empty but full

You can try
To pull me down
To your level
Ultimately
it only makes
Me rise higher
I don't belong
Where you lie
You cannot have me
You cannot take what
is mine

Tell me you
Remember
Dappling light
Our hands
Finally
Finding each other
Again

Tell me you
Remember
My hand willingly
Given and then
Bound again

Lightning strikes
Where intended
I am not

Returning
for you
again.

Empty Space

The glass full
Greatness achieved
Mark hit
Arrow to target
Accuracy
Soul contract fulfilled
The wave has hit
The shore
with the full
Power of intention
And now the pull back
Water rushing backwards
Over sand
Yanking your feet
Out from under you
While I withdraw
The rest
The rest
The rest
Empty space
Light.

Him

Trauma inviting
a torn soul
Spirit attachment
the divide between
Heart and mind
Love and fear
His citadel

Fragments of your soul
Traded in
an attempt to manage
Your own pain
What does pain justify
True control
is only possible
Through surrender

What is it I see
in those moments
Vertically placed
Steel tubing
a drain
Where your love
Soulful emotion rests
While he uses you
to do his punishing

Does he tell you
He just wants love
He knows
I could never
Love him only you
and so
When he puts
your hands around
my neck
do you know how
he smiles.

Outline

My skin is
Sometimes
Difficult to be in
When you are not
Here to touch
Outline
Trace
Define it.

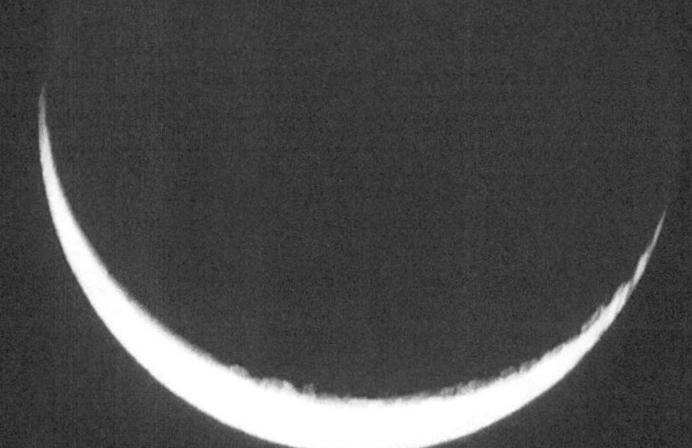

I Wish

I wish
Where I was
going
You could
Go too
The distance between
What the heart wants
and the soul demands.

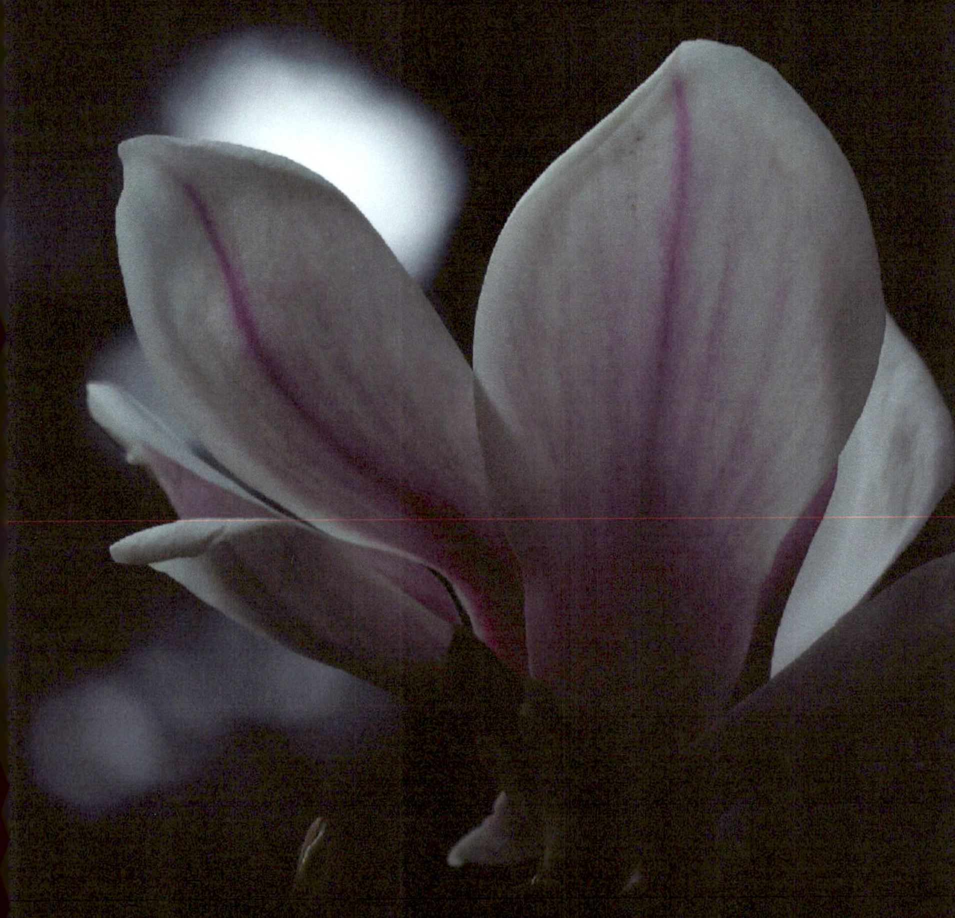

The Only Way, Love

there was
a way out
Love
while still
moving through
Love
invoking integrity
strength
unconditional
Love
instead
you invite
your fears
mistake
Love
as false protection
impure intentions
Love
you've never saved
anything yet
Love
I can
no longer
Love
believe in you
Love.

Cord Cutting

Withdrawn
Cords cut
Gathered and disposed
Was it worth it
Loving you.

Receive

The rope
Between us
I sever
Withdraw
From the flayed ends
Riotous blooms
Dripping in piles
at my feet
A bower
Surrounded by beauty
Reverently they come
I cry
as they pry
my arms open
Filling them
With the flowers
that are
Painful
to receive
Without you
As the giver

The debris
The abandonment
You leaving me here
to rot
Filled my life
With a beauty
and wonder
Astonishment
whatever it was that the
Universe sent you to me
To receive

has been found
I have taken
what you had
To leave
to give.

Rebirth

Did you know
The shadows
You lengthened
Left me
More beautifully
darkened
Reflecting
still further
Light.

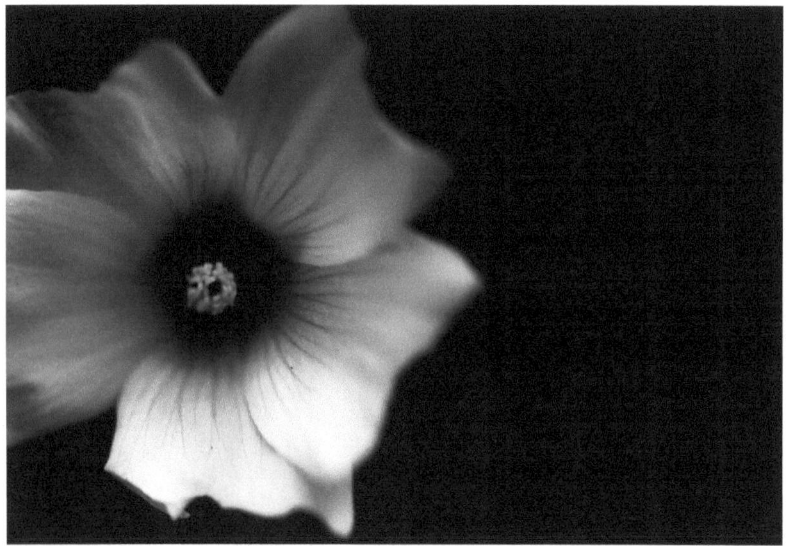

Resolve

The first bloom
Open
Waiting like a cupped hand
The last sword
Slips out softest
Deeper layers of the wound
Already healed
The blood barely
Tops the stamen
Magnolia sighs
She knows this story
This time I will surprise her
Resolve and
Dipping in
Salve to my sorrow.

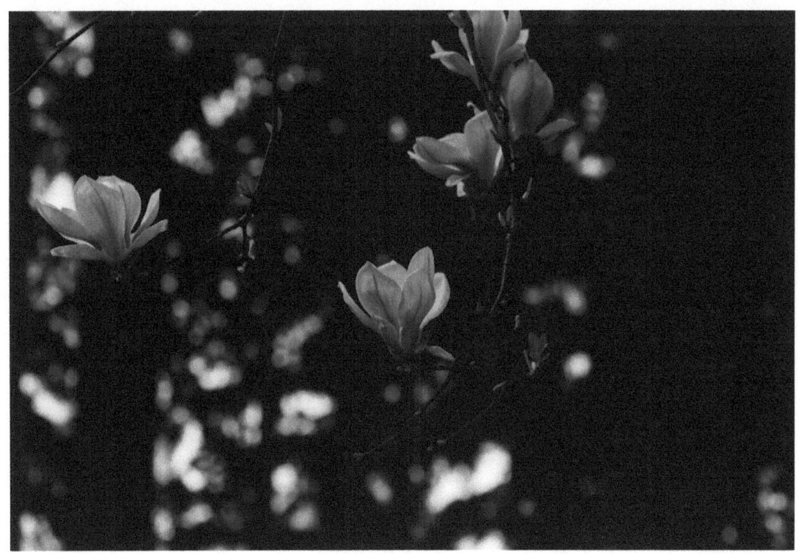

Step Into Your Power

Too long was the journey
Over cliff, through forest
No binding shall ever
Enfold me
Again
The sky is my
Realm now fly
She reminds me.

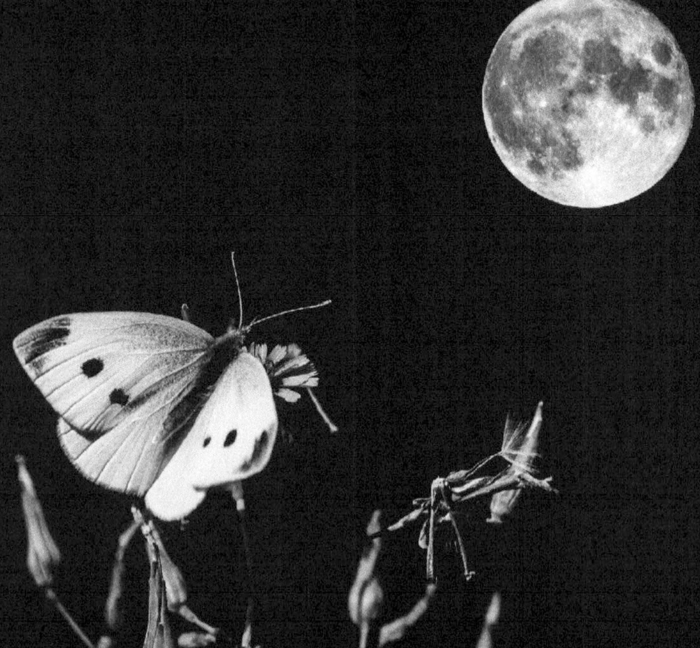

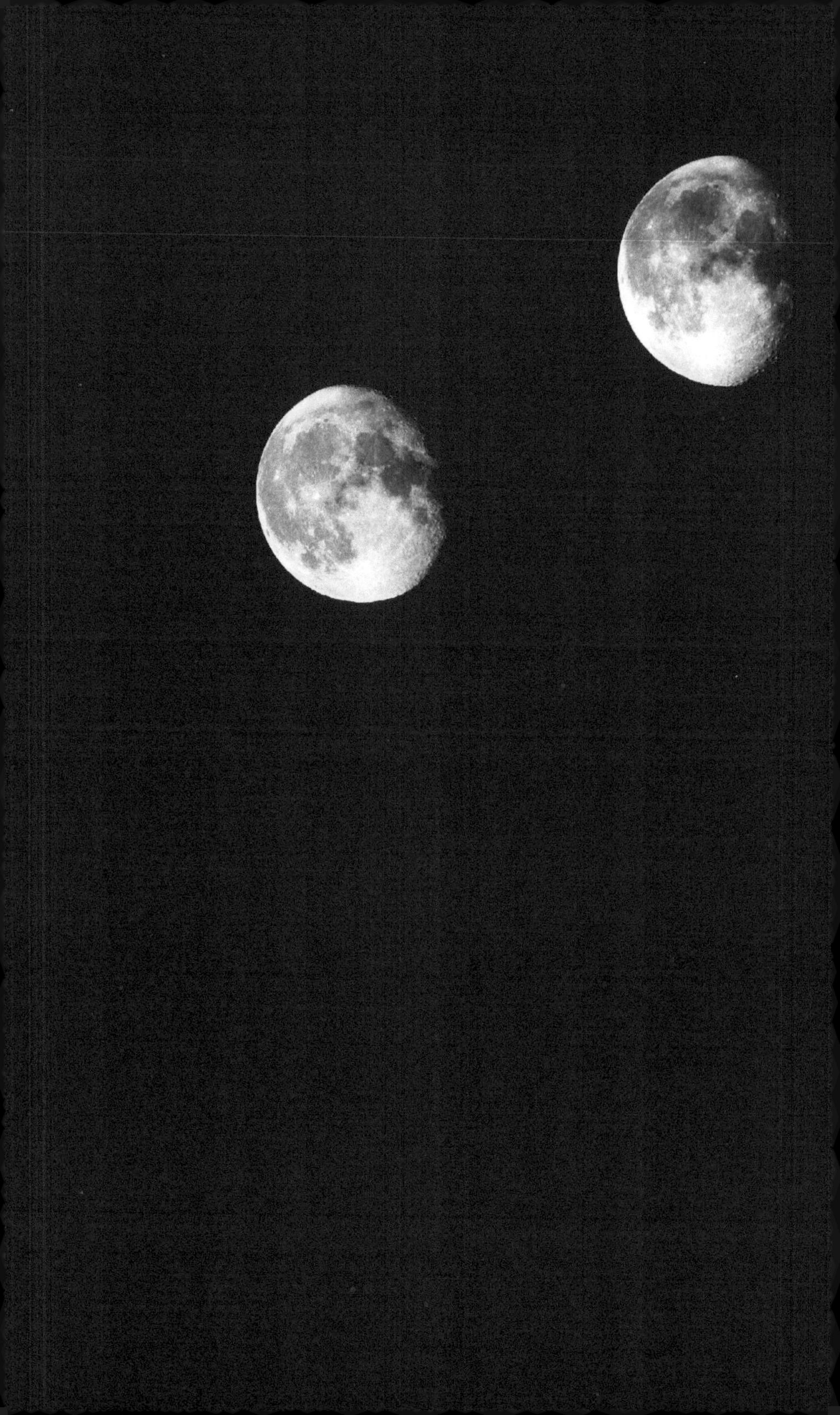

Heal

What I release
Pain how much
Is love worth what is
More difficult than
Choosing yourself over
The person you love
Most

What I keep
Place you
Where I can find you
In stars, fallen leaves
Morning sky and the
Space   between
Breaths

Why I choose
Your energy
Transformed
Resembling potential
Beauty
Lost but always
remembered.

Duality

I love a man
Who has
Another man
Living inside him
Guise of protector
Decrying the weak
Counterpart
Infiltrating doubt
denying reason

I love a man
Who has two men
Willfully
Living inside him
Lover and punisher
I love a man
Whose life is
The battlefield
between
Heart and mind

I love a man
Who is not
A sovereign being
Who bows down in fear
Condemning
Love and life
I love a man
I loved a man.

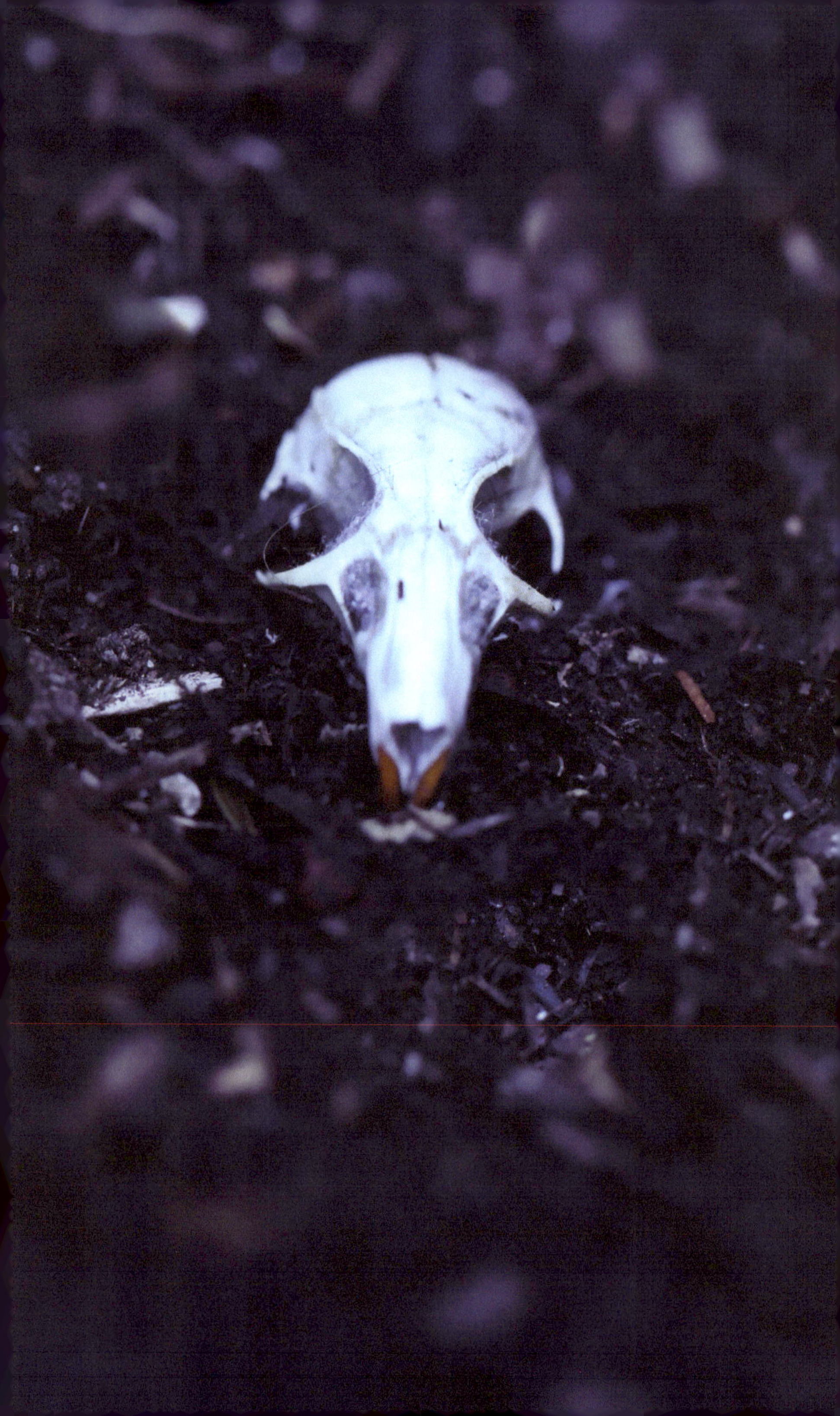

Psychopomp

I know you
Look here
Situationally assess
My feelings in words
I write you think
For you
Likening a soul
To a tree
What is the difference
I kiss mouths
that remind
Me of yours
Let's be clear
I don't
Love you anymore
Stop hoping
Do it now
Fulfill the contract
After the offering
Only then.

Soul Contract

The sun is setting
On our soul
contract
Bells chiming
from far away
Signaling departure

To wolf meadow
where I find you
lifeless
slumped against
a fallen tree

Ultimately
You will prove useful
Even in death
a body returns
nutrients
Feeding the dirt
transformed
placed where you will
be of service.

Divine Shrine

Beyond
A healing
consideration
I don't need to
Know where
What you are
As I've long since
Grown
Accustomed to
other hands
Stronger
Men who pause
Relishing breaths
Between words
worlds
My body mending
Worshipped
Divine shrine
to freedom.

Resources

National Domestic Violence Hotline

Help is available. Speak with someone today.

Hours: 24/7

Languages: English, Spanish and 200+ through interpretation service

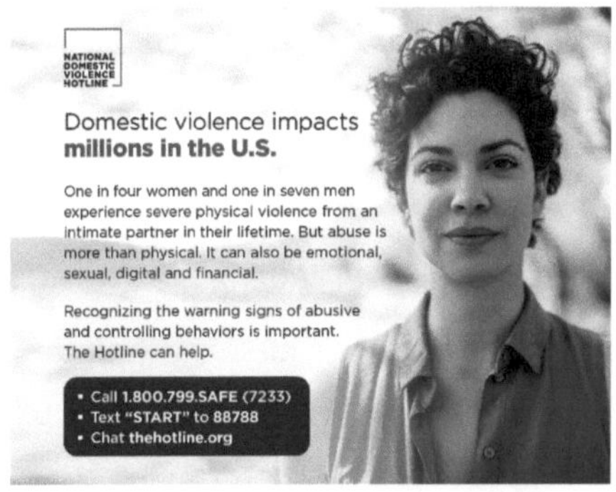

The Verbally Abusive Relationship by Patricia Evans

www.verbalabuse.com

Allies in Change

Allies in Change is a non-profit social activist organization and counseling services center seeking to prevent domestic violence by offering community trainings, education, and outreach to local organizations and the public to raise awareness about domestic violence.

Allies@AlliesinChange.org | (503) 297-7979

About Altered Tarot

r. tanksley is mom of two incredible universes, a celebrated elementary educator of 18 years, and an ardent environmentalist. In poetry, she encapsulates her moments of waxing and waning emotional intensity and, as moon goddess divine, shares insight and clarity with readers. Her work has been published in *Harbinger's Asylum* and explores themes of healing, compassion, and spirituality. She empowers students to explore their intuitions, identities, and values through the practice of poetry. Robyn is proud to call herself a survivor of domestic violence and an advocate for all women experiencing trauma and systemic injustices. She lives in Portland, OR.

k. hiatt loves to spend time in the woods observing and photographing wildlife. She lives in Portland, Oregon with her husband Jim, their 4 children, 2 dogs and cat. She is an adored elementary teacher of 16 years, inspiring her students to express themselves through art.

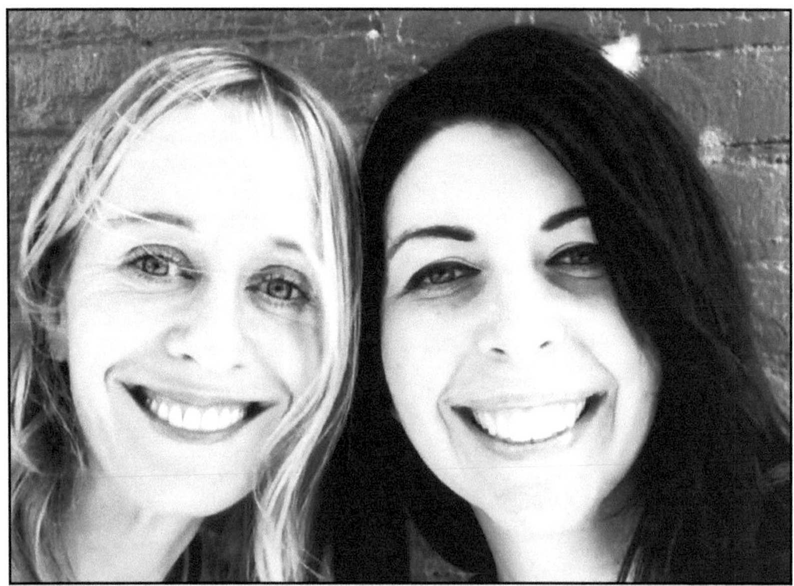

Learn more at alteredtarot.com